ISBN 978-1-332-11989-9
PIBN 10287322

For support please visit www.forgottenbooks.com

1 MONTH OF
FREE
READING

at

www.ForgottenBooks.com

By purchasing this book you are eligible for one month membership to ForgottenBooks.com, giving you unlimited access to our entire collection of over 700,000 titles via our web site and mobile apps.

To claim your free month visit:

www.forgottenbooks.com/free287322

Similar Books Are Available from
www.forgottenbooks.com

STANLEY MANUFACTURING CO.

MAKERS OF

oot and Shoe Machiner

No. 117 LINCOLN STREET,

BOSTON, MASS.

U. S. A.

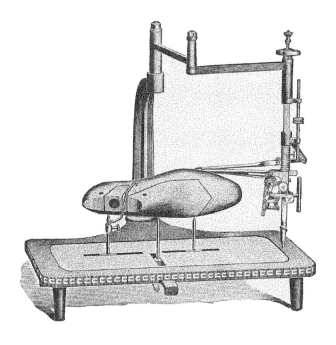

PATTERN DRAFTING MACHINE.

OF THE BLACKINGS,

CEMENTS, DRESS-
INGS, STAINS, &c.,
USED BY THE BOOT
AND SHOE MAN-
UFACTURERS OF
THE WORLD ARE

MANUFACTURED ᴮʸ ᴛʜᴇ

BOSTON BLACKING CO

Boston, Mass., U. S. A.

———

ENGLISH BRANCH: LEICESTER, ENGLAND.

———

GERMAN AGENTS: KEATS MACHINERY CO., Frankfort a. M.
FRENCH AGENTS: A. HERMANN & CO., Paris, France.

DESIGNING, CUTTING
AND GRADING

OT AND SHOE PATTER

AND COMPLETE MANUAL FOR
THE STITCHING ROOM,

BY AN EXPERT OF THIRTY YEARS.

THOROUGHLY ILLUSTRATED.

BOSTON, U.S.A.
PRESS OF SUPERINTENDENT AND FOREMAN.
1899.

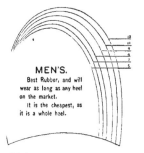

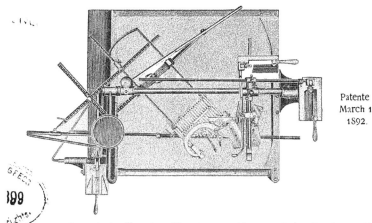

CONTENTS.

Contents. — *Continued.*

INTRODUCTION.

It is my purpose to write of and fully illustrate the art of designing and cutting boot and shoe patterns so that uppers cut therefrom may fit the lasts perfectly. I shall constantly keep in mind the operations to be performed on the uppers in the fitting room, in the lasting room, and in all other departments of the factory. My constant aim will be to economize stock in the cutting room, to save time and labor in the fitting room, and to produce patterns from which, with our modern factory methods, may be made shoes that fit well, look well, and are full of that more or less definite something which we call "style."

I shall also treat at full length the various methods of grading in sizes and widths with the different grading machines, comparing the results. I shall describe the various methods of hand grading, fully illustrating all with carefully drawn diagrams.

This is an undertaking of considerable magnitude, and although I have been for the last thirty-five years almost continuously travelling throughout the United States and Canada, visiting repeatedly almost every boot and shoe manufacturer in America, except where very heavy goods only are made, instructing manufacturers, their superintendents or foremen, and gathering points for myself, I nevertheless hesitate at undertaking a task that is so filled with detail and so difficult to make intelligible.

I am aware that there are publications on the subject of boot and shoe patterns for which large prices are asked, but I never yet have seen one by which the ordinary person can, without previous training, become a thorough pattern maker or designer, capable of doing practical work in a shoe factory.

I will commence with women's, misses' and children's boots and low cuts, heel and spring heel. I will treat these in McKay's, welts and turns individually. Men's, boys' and youth's will follow, and all will be illustrated with the necessary diagrams. The writer will use his best endeavors to the end that the information may be of such a character that any person mechanically inclined can from it and the necessary practical experience become proficient.

C. B. HATFIELD.

ROCHESTER, N. Y., October, 1897.

DESIGNING, CUTTING AND GRADING BOOT AND SHOE PATTERNS.

CHAPTER I.

MOULDING THE LAST.

It is premised that we start with a proper last. Let us begin with a woman's McKay sewed circular vamp dongola buttoned boot. To properly mould the last is the first operation. Men do, or try to do, this in different ways. In one a piece of upper leather is moistened, drawn over the last, rubbed down and moulded until it fits closely to the last at every point. It is fastened in this position with tacks and remains on the last until thoroughly dried. Then the leather is cut away around the edge of the last where the edge of the insole would come. Then a straight line is cut from the centre of the cone, at the top, to the centre of the toe, and up and down the centre of the heel. The leather comes off the last in two parts, one from the inside, the other the outside, in shell-like appearance. Partly by moistening and partly by slashing the edges these shells are flattened out. The mean average of these two pieces of leather, on paper, is supposed to give a proper mould. Such a mould may do for very coarse, heavy work, but it is not sufficiently accurate for fine work.

Another method proceeds on similar lines with heavy drill or canvas, using shellac to fasten to the last. The result is no better.

Positive proof that neither of these is the correct method is found as follows: Let two different people mould the same last by either method, and compare results.

The simplest, most positive, most practical method was invented by myself nineteen years ago—a method so simple and so correct that when followed out and according to instructions, ten different people in ten different localities will all arrive at identical results.

Cut a piece of manila paper, about the substance of that used by professional pattern makers, into shape approximating the shape of one-half the last, leaving it large enough to cover one side. Next draw a line with a pencil from the centre of the comb of the last to the centre of the toe on top, or as near centre ∿s the eye locates. If it be a welt or turn last, line the last where the edge of the sole would come on the shank. Lay the last on its side, tack the paper to side of the heel, about half way up, and swing the toe of the paper up and down until it is in the right position. (See diagram 1.)   Then tack it to the last at the

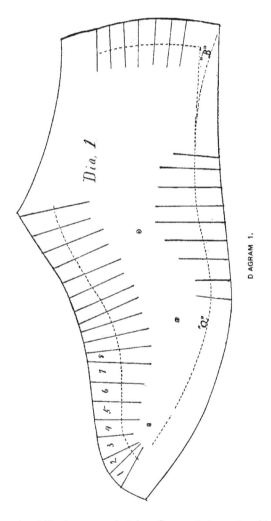

ball, and, while the paper is lying flat, tack it to the side of the toe, springing the paper neither up nor down on the last, but allowing it to lie naturally, thus preserving the toe spring of the last. This is verv essential: Use as many tacks as vou choose, but do not twist the paper. Next slash the paper as seen in diagram 1. While the last is lying upon a support, rub the lower edge along the line of the sole with a dirty handled knife, a bit of lead, or anything which, being rubbed along the projection of the corner of the sole of the last, will leave a black mark. See dotted line "A," diagram 1. Care must be taken at the lower back corner of the heel, or the paper will lift from the last and cause a downward curved mark, as shown by dotted line B, diagram 1.

When you have thus determined the line of sole, bring each piece as marked with the small numerals on diagram 1,—1-2-3-4-5, etc., successively, one at a time, to the line already drawn through the middle of the last. Mark with pencil or cut with knife on the line until the whole is finished. After this operation pull out the tacks and remove

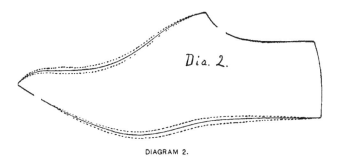

DIAGRAM 2.

paper. Proceed in same way with the other side of the last and another piece of paper. This gives you both sides of the last on paper.

To obtain the mean average of these two sides—and by that means to calculate what is necessary to cover one-half of the last—mark on another piece of manila paper, around first one of these half moulds, and then the other, in the same relative position on each. See diagram 2. After this cut out your mould, splitting all differences, or dividing between the lines with your eye.

You now have what is called the mould of the last, which will be in this instance a woman's 4-C McKay sewed.

CHAPTER II.

The next step will be to get a shell or complete outside standard for an ordinary button boot, side lace, or any boot that is seamed both front and back in the leg. Select a piece of paper large enough to make a standard and place the last mould on it. Set a pair of dividers for McKay work, say five-eighths inch, and draw around the bottom of the last mould. This gives sufficient stock for lasting and

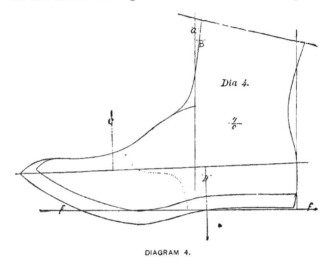

DIAGRAM 4.

covering the insole. It may take a little less or a little more, the amount depending largely on the stock and the factory. What is just enough for one factory is not enough for another, owing mostly to the way the laster uses his pincers. These things must be decided by the pattern maker, for he has the opportunity to observe the results of his efforts; and any one who proposes to become proficient in designing must have a good store of sound common sense and be willing to use it at any and all times as against theory.

The next step is to get the floor line. See diagram 4, F F. This is done by measuring down from about the centre of the heel the height that the breast of the heel is to be, in this instance three-fourths of an inch; and from this point draw a line by means of a straight edge to the ball of the mould. This represents the floor that the shoe will rest on when finished, only it would be the thickness of the sole lower.

Now erect a perpendicular line from the floor by
means of a right angled square, just touching the extreme
rear point of the mould at the heel, and extending upwards
say seven and a half inches. Then get the curve for the
back of the leg by means of a curve, drawn by your eye,
from the top, or near the top of the back of the heel of the
mould, to a point six inches upward from the bottom of the
mould and three-eighths of an inch backward from the ver-
tical. Some manufacturers of ladies' fine shoes have
adopted the leg curve for ladies' shoes, shown in diagram
No. 5.

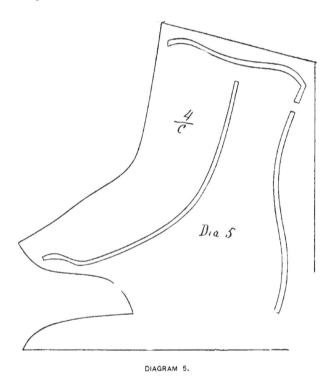

DIAGRAM 5.

If you do not have this curve, measure across the
smallest part of the ankle, or where it curves in the greatest, one-half the girth measurement of the ball of the last;
then add one-eighth inch for the two seams, front and
back, and erect another perpendicular from the floor. See
diagram 4, line A.

This being a 4-C, the standard height in America at
the back is six inches from the rand up. The height at the
front should be more, as the eye will tell you, so draw a
straight line across the top, slanting up at the front. Where
this line intersects the perpendicular measure back from
the perpendicular the same amount of space as the top of

the back line lays back of the back perpendicular. From this point in front draw a straight line to the point of measurement that you have across the ankle. See diagram 4, line "B."

This finishes the leg except the curve at the throat, which, unless you have some fixed curve, you must put in with your eye, striking the comb of the last.

Now, using a size stick, get the length of the last. As is quite generally known all ladies' lasts nowadays are made at least one size longer than standard measure in America, so that size four would draw five sizes on the size stick. Consequently our present experiment draws five sizes. It is now necessary to add 4½ sizes to the length of the pattern over the length of the last, from extreme bulge of heel to extreme point of toe, to make it long enough to last. In this case the extreme length of the standard would be 9½ sizes.

It is better to end the toe of the standard on a curve such as would be desirable in a seam to toe or "gipsy" cut, such as side lace congress, gipsy, button, etc. See diagram 4.

Now draw a horizontal line from the point of the toe to the extreme bulge of the heel, and with a pair of dividers divide into three equal parts. See diagram 4; lines "C," "D."

By means of a square draw down from the horizontal line at rear point of intersecting third, and upward from first third. See diagram 4.

The centre of the shank on a size 4 is seven-eighths of an inch ahead of the back perpendicular line drawn from the third, D, and this is the place at which to end the curve of a circular vamp except in extreme cases. The length of the vamp on top in a finished shoe, size 4, varies according to taste, but at the present time it is desired to be from three and five-eighths to four and one-fourth inches. The shape of the curve is entirely a matter of taste.

The standard may now be dissected for various styles of shoes, but before proceeding further get out a standard for a woman's spring heel 4-C; the only difference being the height of the heel, showing that the floor line, F, must be obtained from the shoe as it will be finished. See diagram 10.

It will be observed that the curve at the back of the leg is somewhat straighter in a spring heel shoe, and that the throat curve is somewhat sharper. This is because the foot is in a different position relatively to the leg than when it is in a heel shoe.

Now notice diagram 11. This represents a standard got out from a last made to carry a heel one and three-fourths inches high at the breast. The diagram shows very plainly a difference in the curve at the back of the leg; it is much sharper; the throat curve is straighter; and in these particulars it is just the reverse of a spring heel shoe.

A continuation of the back curve in its present posi-

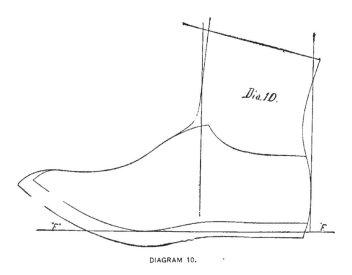

DIAGRAM 10.

tion, and a similar continuation of the front line upward will give a good high leg.

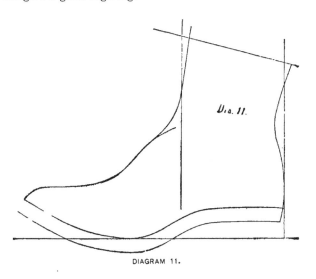

DIAGRAM 11.

Diagram 12 shows the standard with the curved line of the vamp, the curved line of the front of the quarter where the vamp is stitched and the lap that is required. The amount of lap required is not uniform. In some factories more is required than in others. Some factories require one-fourth inch only, others three-eighths inch. It is best in all cases to cut paterns with the lap that has been in use in the stitching room of a factory. No advantage is to be gamed by arbitrarily changing it.

For convenience of getting out the pattern, cut the piece of paper representing the lap out of the standard. Always make the lap for a plain vamp, and never allow for beading, provided it be a beaded vamp, in the opening. It is very easy to add the beading to the vamp when getting it out. This serves to prevent confusion, for the question

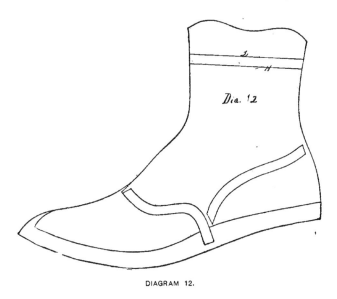

DIAGRAM 12.

sometimes arises as to whether the standard was for plain or beaded vamp.   Diagram 12 also shows a foxing laid out, with the lap, at bottom of quarter.   Again referring to diagram 12, you will notice near the top of the leg two lines drawn across, one representing the lower edge of the top facing, marked "H," the other representing the top edge of the cloth lining, "L." This standard is made with a wave top, for the purpose of getting out the first standard button boot with an even bead around the edge of the upper where it is beaded.

CHAPTER III

To cut a ladies' dongola button boot pattern : first, cut a piece of paper large enough to fold in the centre. Cut two quarters at one cutting. They are then necessarily exactly alike, the second one not increased in size as it would be by marking around one to get the other. Mark around the standard to get your quarters. Cut out. This will of course leave both the same size. Commencing at the bottom end (see diagram 13) at "C," cut away for small quar-

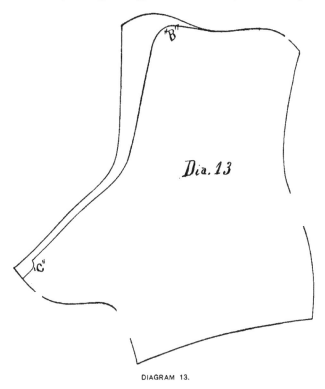

DIAGRAM 13.

ter along the instep line three-sixteenths of an inch until the curve of throat is reached, then cut away about one-fourth of an inch. Measure in at the top of the quarter, say three-fourths of an inch from the front and finish from the top of throat curve to that point. The fly or button lap, as it may be termed when the shoe is finished, will cover that portion of the small quarter at the top. It will save stock to cut it straight out from the lowest point of top and then round the corner, as in diagram 13, letter "B."

BUTTONS IN RIGHT POSITION.

Permit a digression at this point and reference to the greatest source of trouble in a button boot, viz, the correct positions of the buttons. By looking at the shoes in a lasting room in a great many shoe factories, it will be found that the front seam on the instep of the last is very crooked. Oftentimes it appears to run away to the inside. The bottom end of the button fly between the vamp and the first button bulges up, showing a bad fullness or wrinkle. Examination of the line of the small quarter under the button fly shows that it is from three- eighths to five-eighths of an inch below the front seam, having been drawn down there by lasting. All this is the result of the buttons not having been put on in their proper places to hold the small quarter up where it belongs.

It is the height of folly to undertake to cut patterns for button boots to the one-thirty-second of an inch, and then allow by carelessness, neglect, or through ignorance, the operative in the stitching room to put buttons on and not have them in their proper places. It may be further said that there is more trouble caused by want of attention to the proper placing of buttons on button boots than by any one thing that transpires in their manufacture. See that every button is put on in its proper position.

A great many pattern makers, professional and amateur, cut away the small quarter down the instep line only one-sixteenth of an inch at the bottom to one-eighth of an inch near the throat curve. This may be correct in theory, but a dongola boot will not fit if cut in this manner. The shoe will not be even at the bottom edges, when folded carefully along the instep seam and held by the thumb and finger, the bottom edges drawn down by the other hand. The out or button side of the upper will extend below the inside from one-eighth to three-eighths of an inch, unless when vamping, the lower end of the small quarter is lapped clear by the centre seam all the way up to the throat, while the positions for the buttons are being marked.

Now this applies to a dongola button boot; but if cut from heavy grain, split, buff, or anything of that kind, the small quarter should be cut away down the instep line from one-fourth of an inch to five-sixteenths of an inch.

In fitting the small quarter of a button boot the remark is often made, "Why, the small quarter beads off a seam." But it does not. Only another theory. Look over a lot of shoes in the factory ready to be vamped. It will be found that the cloth lining does all the beading and simply adds on to the small quarter down the front line. There are a few factories in the United States where the beading is done evenly down that line, but they are but few, and the prices paid for that work are correspondingly high.

Starting up the front of a small quarter three-eighths of an inch back, cut away three-sixteenths of an inch down to the front end of the small quarter. See "C," diagram 13. This is done for the purpose of giving the operator who closes the lining on to the outside a guide to work from,

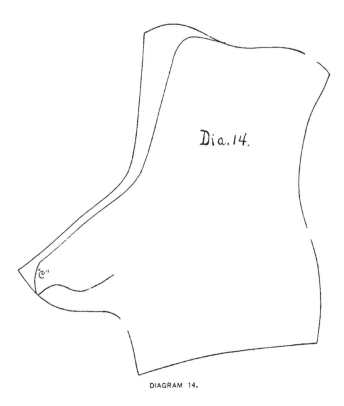

DIAGRAM 14.

as well as to accomplish a purpose in closing the toe of the lining. When cutting a pattern for a very cheap shoe, it will be well to round the front end of the small quarter clear down to the place where it meets the lower end of the button fly. See diagram 14, "C." This would save stock and take the thickness out from under the lower end of the button fly and vamp, as shown at "C," diagram 14.

THE CLOTH LINING AND BUTTON FLY.

The next step will be to get a cloth lining. It is preferable in all cases where the cost of production will allow to cut two lining patterns, one for the full quarter, the other cut away to match the small quarter. Leave on about one-twelfth of an inch down the front, so that the quarter may be set back a little on the lining. The cloth, not being so liable to fray out, gives the operator (generally termed the "closer on" or the "second closer") a guide to stitch by, and does not require her to use her judgment as to the amount of material to be trimmed away down the front of the lining on the small side. In other words, she is not obliged to gauge the distance back from the edge of

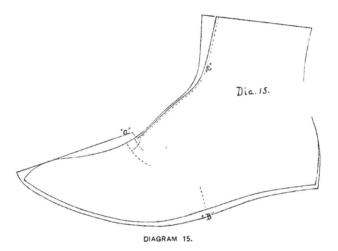

Dia. 15.

DIAGRAM 15.

the lining with her eye. If left to one lining pattern and the judgment of the operator, where eye measurement is used entirely, the next operator is very liable to use a different eye measurement. In consequence, the shoe coming from one operator may have smooth linings through the legs while that from the next operator wrinkles.

Linings are fitted with what is now generally adopted as the regulation cloth seam, one-fourth inch. If a greater seam allowance is required add the difference; if less, take off the difference.

Fold a piece of paper large enough to cut both linings. Lay the standard diagram 12 upon it and mark around, commencing at the cross line "L," going entirely around the standard, up the other side and again stop at "L." As is understood, this pattern is for a ladies' dongola McKay-sewed. So the pattern will be for a McKay lining. After having marked around the standard, by means of a pair of dividers, add one-eighth of an inch all around the bottom of this, to give material equivalent for the stretch in the upper obtained by lasting; and notwithstanding so much has already been allowed more must be added in the shank. See diagram 15, "A."

While the standard is still in position, mark through the lap of the vamp at the top; also at front of quarter. This supplies a guide for the ending of the toe seam, as that is desired to come up three-eighths of an inch back of the front of the quarter, so as to match where the "closer on" has stopped at the notch made in the front of the quarter.

Dia 140

DIAGRAM 140.

By doing this, there will be no hole left at the back of the toe seam in the lining.

The majority of factories at the present time will find their patterns cut on cheap work in such a manner that the "closer on" runs down to about where she considers right in stitching the outside on to the lining and then shoots off. Since the toe seam of the lining generally commences at the end of the quarter there is a bad hole left open at this point. Likewise in a majority of factories making a finer grade of goods the "closer on" stitches the outside on to the lining clear down to the end of the quarter, when the shoes are passed to "table girls," who rip them up a little so that the linings may be turned back in vamping. This also leaves a bad hole at the end of the toe seam.

Diagram 140 represents a lining running to the top where no top facing is required.

Vamping through linings may be considered here. One can see that by this method of cutting patterns it costs nothing to turn the linings back, for no table hands are needed on the uppers. The patterns are cut so as to go together by the edge of the lining and the outside in all shoes of whatever description. An experience of years has shown that it is absolutely impossible to vamp through the linings of button boots and get smooth linings. Part of the case may come fairly smooth, but others from the same case will be wrinkled, because the vamper draws them unevenly, some not quite far enough forward, others too far. The latter fault causes a tight heel lining. A shoe with a tight heel lining, no matter how much time and trouble is spent in lasting, will never draw well. By referring to diagram 15, it will be noticed that the toe of the standard ends at a point; therefore allow your lining to be about one-eighth inch longer than the standard. Strike the top line of the toe seam and have the front end of it cut a little below the standard at the highest point back, three-eighths of an inch from the front of the quarter, as shown in the standard. Raise three-sixteenths of an inch above the standard a short perpendicular, which gives the top line of toe seam. See diagram 15, "A." Cut under about one-eighth of an inch at the bottom, back of the lining, for allowance for counter, from nothing to the height of two and one-fourth inches. This completes the large lining.

To obtain the small lining, place the small quarter in its proper position on the lining and mark around the front of it, leaving one-twelfth of an inch down the front of the quarter, "C," and at the bottom end of the quarter, or three-eighths of an inch above. Cut up to the top to match the large side of lining, "A." If no seam is desired in the toe of the lining, it would be well to cut off the three-sixteenths of an inch which has been added for the seam "A," and only make a notch to guide the operator in fitting. However, the cloth is there, and it seems a great waste not to toe seam and get the benefit of the strength of the cloth across the vamp and ball of the foot.

The next step will be to get the button fly, or as it is termed in some places, the button lap. It has been the custom with many to give the fly quite a spring when cutting the pattern in a way to make it hug closely to the shoe on the scalloped edge.

Try one with no spring, having the small quarter cut away according to directions, and put the buttons on the shoe in just the correct positions. The result is likely to be very pleasing.

To get the fly, mark round the large quarter front, top and bottom. If you have no curve for fly, take about the middle of the leg at the top for a start and bring down in

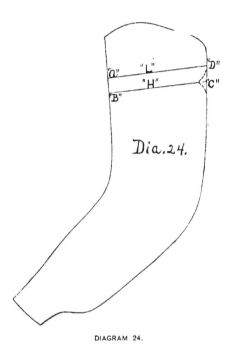

DIAGRAM 24.

as correct a sweep as possible, until you come almost to vamp line. Then finish from bottom up. See diagram 24.

CHAPTER V

To cut a circular plain vamp, place the standard, diagram 12, on a piece of paper, mark around the forward part of it and back to the curve of back of vamp. This makes ready to get out the one-half vamp.

The length of finishing the vamp at toe is to be just the same as point of standard. Draw a straight line on the top going one-sixteenth of an inch below at the highest point on toe, "A"; also the same at end of curve of back of vamp, "B." This will be equivalent for the seam that will be taken off the large quarter. See diagram 16.

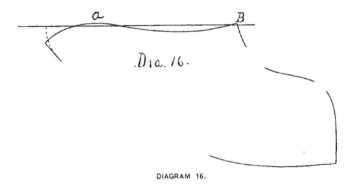

DIAGRAM 16.

Fold the paper at line "A"-"B," and cut out the half vamp. This half vamp, if exactly duplicated in another half, will make a whole vamp, as shown in diagram 17.

This vamp gives too much stock all around the bottom where it is lasted, and the laster has much work to last it in. When the shoe is finished wrinkles are likely to show in the shank. The leather is drawn forward by the pincers in lasting, and everything except the bottom edge of the upper is stretched so as to make the shoe hug the last. Consequently, the shoe shows a fullness all around the bottom. This may be remedied by cutting the vamp, sprung down, so that it touches the toe of the last rather hard at first. After it is pulled over the last and fastened with the usual toe tacks, the next pulls on the sides of the ball bring the stock over the sole, leaving less to be "worked in." The best method for cutting the vamp is as follows:—

Place diagram 16, after it has been cut out, on a piece of paper large enough to cut a vamp. Mark around it, and instead of folding the paper on the top straight line,

"A-B," drop the front of the line, say one-half inch to "C-D." Score the paper so it will fold there; then fill out the

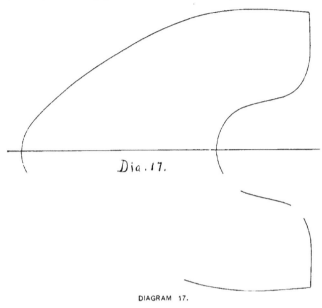

DIAGRAM 17.

toe at E by placing diagram 16 on the folded line. This will give sufficient stock to last well. In diagram 18 this

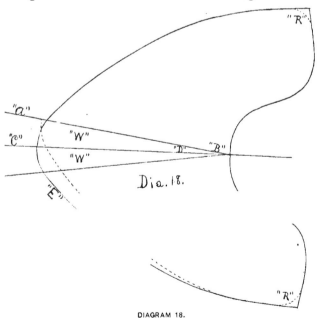

DIAGRAM 18.

method is illustrated. This one point has a great deal to do with the draught of a shoe. Observe that the wedge-

shaped piece, "W" "W," is cut from the toe, effecting a
saving in stock, besides preventing shank wrinkles.   Of
course this has a tendency to throw up the back of the
vamp from the last and foot, and if second lasting is omit-
ted this is likely to show some in the finished shoe.   In
that case the production will be of such a cheap character
that it will probably make no difference.   It does prevent
the vamp and quarter lap seam from pressing hard upon
the foot.

Referring to diagram 18, notice how the corners
are rounded off at "R." This is for a double purpose.   In
the first place, the cutter will go around the corners without stopping.   One must always cut by, or over, or beyond,
a corner to cut it clear.   Cutting beyond wastes stock,

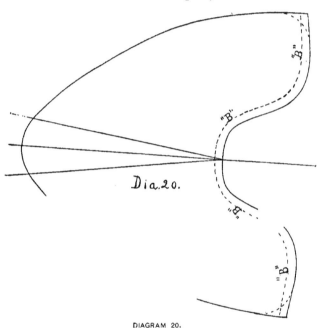

DIAGRAM 20.

while the round corner does no injury, as the bottom of the
vamp laps on to the quarter sufficiently to cover it.

Diagram 20 shows the same vamp as shown in diagram 18, three-sixteenths, on the back for beading or folding, dotted line "B B B B." It is rounded still more than
diagram 18, but when the vamp is folded and ready to be
stitched on to the quarter, there will be just about five-sixteenths of an inch left on the round, so it will do no harm, as
the lap seam of quarter will cover it.   There is a saving in
the amount of leather when cutting vamps as shown in diagram 20 over that shown in diagram 17.   The upper
draws much better on account of the toe being sprung
down.   The foreman who has a fair fund of common sense

and is at all mechanically inclined, will have no trouble
folding the vamp so it will be easy for the vamper to guide
it in lap, as dotted line shows where to commence and finish at the rounded corners. This is essential, as, if the operators on the skiving and folding machines are not properly instructed, they are apt to skive and fold around the
place cut round to save stock, and this would not leave a
point for vamper.

ROUNDING OFF CORNERS.

Shoes are produced now with so little per pair profit
to the average manufacturer that any little point of saving

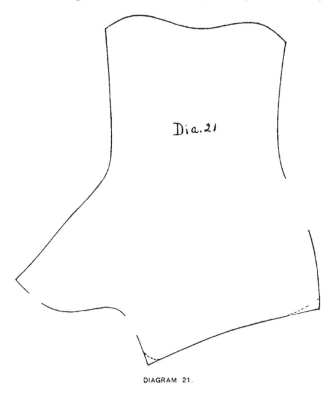

Dia. 21

DIAGRAM 21.

is really worth while. Look at diagram 21; notice the two
bottom corners of the quarters. This idea is in practice
in a large factory producing ladies' shoes. The manufacturer stated that it saves a good deal in a year, both in
stock and time of cutting, for the cutter does not have to
stop at the corners. Not having so much to turn in, it
is easier to last at the heel seat. Numerous tests proved
that the manufacturer was right.

At "A," diagram 22, the bottom of the quarter is
rounded off to save stock. It also acts as a guide for the
stitcher. This may represent either plain or beaded foxing.

Diagram 23 represents a foxing rounded at the lower corners to save stock, showing by dotted line, "A," the allowance for beading or folding. It is cut off at "C" di-

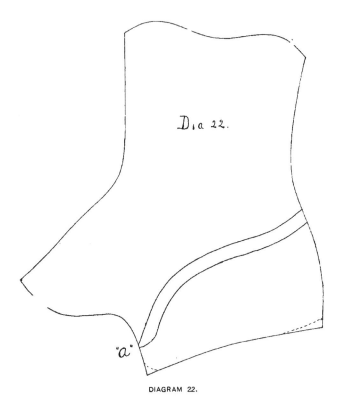

DIAGRAM 22.

agonally to prevent a lump forming in folding. All cutting that is necessary should be done in the cutting room when

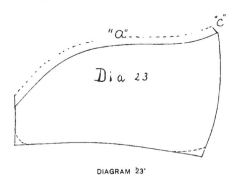

DIAGRAM 23'

the shoes are cut, so that the operator in the stitching room will not have occasion to use scissors and judgment.

The parts attending the folding of the foxing, closing of the front and back seams, putting the foxings on and staying the shoes, should receive close attention. A gauge should be permanently attached to the machine for guiding the work as to the depth of seams. It will hardly be necessary to say that the smaller the seam taken the less lump there will be. The operator should not be allowed to trim with hand shears. Of course, if the seam is rubbed a little previous to staying, it does no harm. A good many manufacturers, however, allow the foot of the staying machine to do all the rubbing.

Close the back and front seams of the quarters. Also fold the foxings and close the back seam. Next stitch foxings on the quarters, after which stay the quarter down the back through foxings and quarter all at one operation. This prevents a double thickness of staying where the fox-

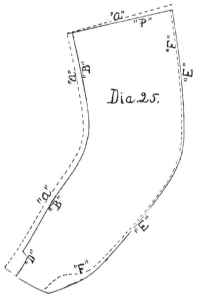

DIAGRAM 25.

ing is lapped on, and really strengthens the shoe at the back seam, the stay being in one piece.

There has been a good deal of complaint about the stitching of the edge of the foxings unless they are first cemented on. This is not necessary if the machine is properly adjusted. Use a sharp feed, relieving the strain on the presser foot.

Referring back again to diagrams 17, 18, 19, 20, cut vamps each way and test the saving of stock. When cutting vamps after diagrams 18 and 19, throw the wings of the vamp out towards the centre of the skin at every opportunity, for the wings, or the toe of the vamp, or any corner of a quarter, will turn and cut almost clean the stock left from the throat of the vamp.

After getting out the fly, prick through at "A," "B," corresponding with the lines, "L," "H," diagram 12, for the purpose of having the same point at that place for width of top facing and height of lining and "C." Point off where the bottom of the first scallop will come as place to finish the bottom of top facing, so that lower edge of it will come at the juncture of the first two scallops, thus preventing it from ever coming into the button-hole. Use this fly to mark around for the fly lining, which in this case is cut solid from leather, as illustrated in diagram 25.

. Dotted line "A" represents the mark around the front of the fly. This fly being solid leather, is set back about three-sixteenths of an inch on the cloth lining, as illustrated in diagram 26.

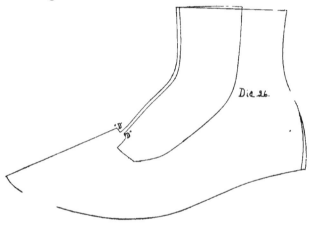

·DIAGRAM 26.

In taking the regulation one-fourth inch seam in the cloth lining, the leather fly lining being so set back, only requires one-sixteenth inch seam. Take the three-sixteenths inch from the sheep fly lining pattern, so that the curves will come right. This gives line "B," diagram 25. Then cut away the bottom at "D" so as to give the operator a guide in fitting the shoe (see "D," diagram 26), and to allow the lining to be thrown back in vamping without any hand shearing. Slip the fly back until the front strikes the line "B," diagram 25, so as to get width at "F E," and mark around as dotted line, "F F." Add one-sixteenth inch, as per line "E E." Measuring from the bottom by means of the fly around the line "F F," it will be found that top dotted line "A" which had been laid out runs too far up and would make the lining too long at that place. Prick through diagram 24 at "D." This gives line "P," diagram 25, the correct one.

CHAPTER VI.

In diagram 27 is made a fly lining, the front part of which is cut from cloth and the button hole piece from

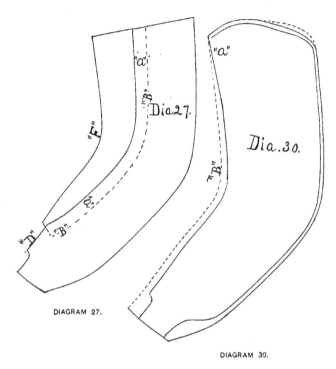

DIAGRAM 27.

DIAGRAM 30.

sheep. This cloth "snipe" is closed on to the leather at seam "A," dotted line "B" showing the lap, and, being

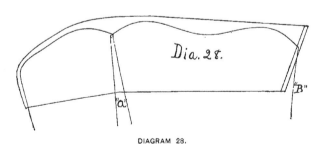

DIAGRAM 28.

cloth, is stitched on evenly at the front edge of the cloth lining; but when the stitch reaches the intersection of the cloth and leather at the bottom "D," it will take but one sixteenth off from the leather at that point.

With either of the above fly linings use top facings, as shown in diagrams 28 and 29.

Diagram 28 shows the top of the large quarter and the top of the button fly laid out with the necessary spring between fly and quarter at "A" to do away with the surplus

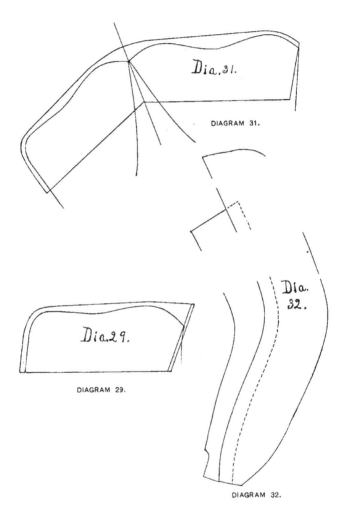

DIAGRAM 31.

DIAGRAM 29.

DIAGRAM 32.

lining or fullness that is sometimes seen. This top facing is cut to be seamed at the back, as by this means it will cut cheaper. At the bottom of the back of the facing (see "B") it is cut under enough to match the one-fourth inch seam in the lining and will absolutely prevent a wrinkle in the lining at this place.

Diagram 29 shows the top facing for the small quarter

and it is shown so plainly that further explanation is not necessary.

Diagram 30 represents a full all leather fly lining. A very few words will explain it. Dotted line represents the edge of the cloth lining, and the top facing is supposed to be stitched on. At "A," diagram 30, swing out on fly lining so that in taking the one-sixteenth inch seam it will reach the end edge of the top facing at "A," causing no lump at that point, giving sufficient room to stitch around the edge on to the quarter. In using whole leather fly lining as shown in diagram 30, it will be necessary to use top facing as shown in diagram 31.

A still different style of fly lining is shown in diagram 32, where a sheep button hole piece runs clear to the top

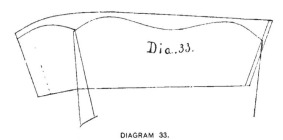

DIAGRAM 33.

of the fly. The "snipe" of cloth is placed even with the front of the cloth lining. The diagram shows the style so plainly that further words seem unnecessary. With a fly lining of this design it will be necessary to get out top facing patterns, according to diagrams 29 and 33.

A POPULAR FOXING.

In diagram 34 is shown another foxing popular at this time. The way of cutting at "A" is presented to assist the operator in folding it. The dotted line shows the finished

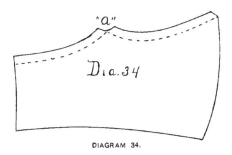

DIAGRAM 34.

edge after folding. In getting this or any other foxing, get out a standard similar to diagram 12, except in so far as changes are made in dissection.

CHAPTER VII.

WHOLE-FOXED OR SEAMLESS VAMPS, CLOTH QUARTERS AND
FLY LININGS.

For whole-foxed or seamless vamps cut standard from diagram 12, except in dissection, and number it diagram 35. Use diagram 12 to get the front of quarter and back of vamp, for by so doing the lining, trimmings and button fly can be used as in diagram 12.

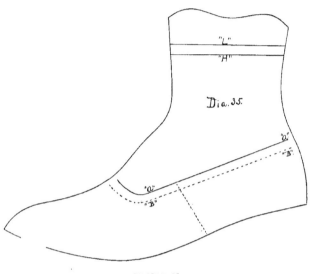

DIAGRAM 35.

Decide the back of vamp at "A," diagram 35, and draw vamp line "A," "A," allowing the usual distance for lap of quarter. Then draw dotted line "B," "B." Cut through on both lines and take out the piece representing the lap.

Mark around the standard diagram 35 and find it in diagram 36, on which draw the line to fold, "A" "A," striking the back line of vamp one-sixteenth inch under the standard line and about on line with the toe of standard. End the vamp the same length at toe as the standard. If the cost of the vamp in cutting were not a factor to be considered, it would be well to drop the toe down at least three-eighths inch, so as to take a gore out of the toe of the vamps. This would reduce the amount of stock around the bottom of the last, but throw the heels of the vamp so as to cost too much to cut.

Some do this and say they can get tongues or button flies out of the centre. But the stock that can be cut into

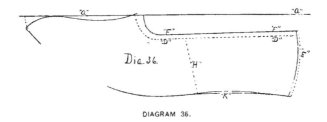

DIAGRAM 36.

a vamp is generally the best of the skin, too valuable to be used in either tongues or flies. This vamp, if cut whole, is generally put on the shoe by a cylinder machine, and when stretched by bead and presser foot, would be too long. Cut it off at the rear from one-eighth to three-sixteenths inch, as seen at "E." The dotted line "D" "D" rep-

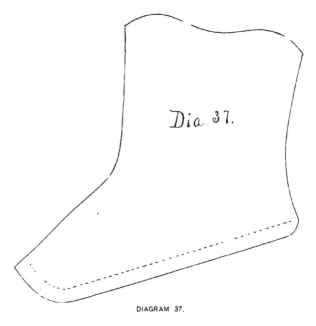

DIAGRAM 37.

resents the vamp as it will be after the folding at line "F" "F" is taken off. The dotted line "H" shows where the vamp is divided into front vamp and foxing. The foxing in this case is generally closed on, and afterwards stayed with a double needle machine, the same as the front and back of the quarters. If desired, the vamp can be cut so as to lap on the foxings, in which case the shoes can be vamped on a flat bed machine, the same as a circular vamp.

It is. as well also, when cutting this whole vamp pat-

tern to allow a little extra at the shank, as shown at "K,"
diagram 36.

Of course, the quarters of this shoe are got from the
standard diagram 35, as in the circular vamp, except if in-
tending to use the linings of diagram 12, use the small

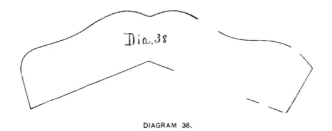

DIAGRAM 38.

quarter obtained from that to cut off an equal amount on
the small quarter of diagram 37.

Now cut and fit a cloth top shoe foxed as shown in
diagram 23. Use the vamp and linings taken from dia-

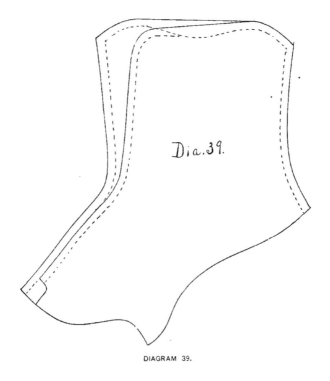

DIAGRAM 39.

gram 12. Here will be shown the advantage of a large
and small lining pattern. A cloth top is fitted easiest when
the lining is fitted "snug," the top facing cut from sheep when
possible and the fly lining cut solid from leather and seal-

loped. This reverses the general way of fitting a leather shoe, and uses the lining of top to fit from, in which case it will be necessary also to have the top facing cut the proper shape, not allowing anything on it for beading as shown in diagram 38.

CLOTH QUARTERS.

To get the cloth quarters, mark around diagram 13, laying off foxing from standard diagram 12. See diagram 39.

Dotted lines show where the leather quarters in diagram 13 come. Since one-fourth inch seam is considered

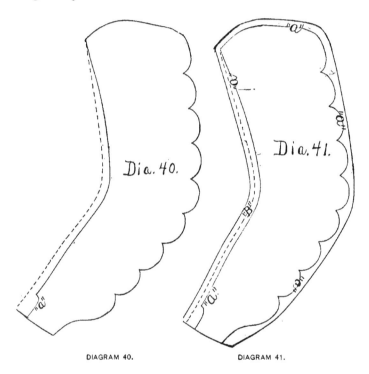

DIAGRAM 40.　　　　　DIAGRAM 41.

best for cloth, and since one-twelfth inch has already been allowed in leather standard diagram, add a little over one-eighth inch here with the dividers.

When fitting this cloth top shoe, use the same linings used in the leather top. So figure that the inside of the shoe will be the same as the leather shoe.

Where it is possible, use a whole button fly lining, when fitting the shoe from the lining.

No matter where the fitting commences, whether on the small quarter or at end of button fly, place the lining about one-eighth of an inch from the edge of the cloth outside, for the small quarter has a guide to place at the end of the lining at the back of the toe seam. Keep the lining one-eighth of an inch from the edge all the way round the shoe. This will give one-eighth of an inch of cloth not trimmed away so the cloth will not fray out in beading.

To get the fly lining use the leather fly. See dotted line, diagram 40, which is the line of the front of the fly, but as this fly lining is of leather, it should be set back on the cloth lining three-sixteenths of an inch, it is cut away from nothing at the top to about three-sixteenths as it runs down. The notch shown at A is to allow the lining to be thrown back in vamping without using hand shears.

Notice that the tops of the cloth quarters, diagram 39, are cut straight from one high point to the other. This costs no more than to cut down to the curve, and is less trouble to cut. It also aids to hold the cloth firmer while being closed on.

Diagram 41 shows the cloth fly with the fly lining lined inside (see lines "A," "A," "A," "A," "A,") and the front of the top facing and cloth lining dotted in (see dotted line B) and also the outside line having the line of the cloth fly The fly lining is scalloped.

This describes the proper fitting of cloth that has not been "backed up." Cloth that is "backed up" may be cut from the leather patterns and fitted as leather shoes are.

CHAPTER VIII.

WOMAN'S DONGOLA BEADED VAMP GYPSY BUTTON BOOT.

Next cut a woman's dongola beaded vamp gipsy button boot. To save time use diagram 12, and by marking around it get diagram 42.

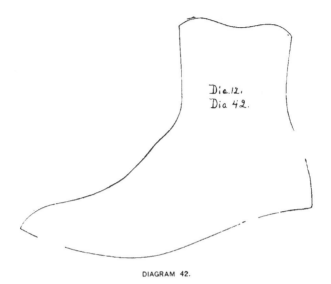

Dia. 12.
Dia 42.

DIAGRAM 42.

It will be apparent to any one why the toe is finished to a point. It is easier to last, as there is less leather to last in than if cut straight.

Use the small quarter made for leather, and the same linings and facings. In equipping a factory, this will reduce the number of patterns. Of course, while saying this. it must be understood that there must be patterns for different styles of lasts, but use the same general standard, provided the shoe to be cut is to be put on the same last. In this day of progress, it probably is useless to discuss the old method of trying to make one set of patterns fit many different styles of lasts. This is all wrong unless the body part of the lasts are similar, and differ only from balls forward.

Some factories use the same set of patterns for all the different styles of lasts. In one of these, the proprietor stated that it cost him 24 cents a pair for fitting button boots. With that system it will never cost less in that factory, and the work is done poorly at that. In this factory six pairs of button boots have been ripped apart and revamped in one day. This manufacturer is a man of large experience in the business, and not long ago wanted the vampers to vamp his shoes without first sewing, or tacking, as they call it, the bottom ends of the quarters, and the operatives said it could not be done and would not try it.

Another factory turning out women's fine shoes had no patterns for cloth shoes, but cut them by "sliding" the leather patterns. The same factory cut all widths shoes, and never had anything but "A," "C," "E," patterns in width. Is it economy?

Dia. 43.

DIAGRAM 43.

If a factory has many styles of lasts and patterns and a wave or a certain curve top is used on many of them, why not, if the top of one set of patterns is correct as to height, and width, hold to that as a standard in getting out other, or new styles, whether they are the same style last or another? By this method the same patterns can be used for top facings, and not only save confusion and liability of wrong cutting, but expense in patterns. If a few top facings be cut wrong by mistake, they may be used on the next case of shoes calling for the same style top.

Before concluding this work some methods of marking and numbering patterns and lasts as adopted by successful manufacturers will be illustrated.

To get button fly for diagram 42, use the button fly
diagram 30, and for back of vamp use diagram 12, which
gives diagram 43.

For a half vamp button as shown in diagram 44, use
standard as per diagram 12 to mark around and get outline,
(see diagram 44) and back of vamp, (see toe of standard
"A"). At B back line of vamp is shown, dotted line "C"
representing the front curve of small quarter under the
vamp. Small quarter is shown all the way up front by
dotted lines which will be recognized at once. Dotted line

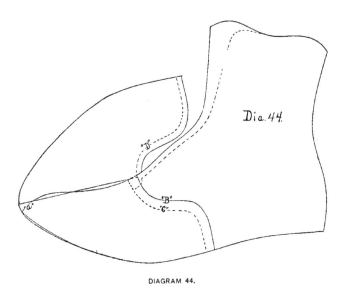

DIAGRAM 44.

"D" represents the line of vamp as it will be after the edge
is folded. Use the small quarter linings and trimmings
from diagram 12.

As to button shoes with whole or seamless vamps. If
the buttons are put a little too far down from their proper
positions, they will cause the vamp to rise up out of a
straight line just below where the quarters strike the last
at the instep. The trouble arises where a large seam is
used in first closing, and the buttons put on a little too
low, and may be remedied by adding a little to the standard along on top the instep line. Common sense must
be used with all systems, and since conditions vary, an
expert must be willing to vary. Just so in the dropping
of the toe of the vamp. Conditions and results must govern without regard to theory. But putting the buttons

on in their correct positions is a positive rule, and safe to be relied on under all conditions.

A few words about beading. After the shoe is "first closed," "stayed" and the outside is "closed on" to the linings, observe the following words about "second closing" on the scallops:

In the first place in a good many factories the scalloping is done so poorly that it is almost no guide for the "closer on." The shape entirely depends on her skill. In such factories, if the operator has learned, when first starting at that branch, to swing the shoe in a steady, even curve as it is stitched and trimmed at the same time, and to make a very sudden sharp turn at the bottom of the scallop she will get nice round scallops, as shown in diagram 45, in-

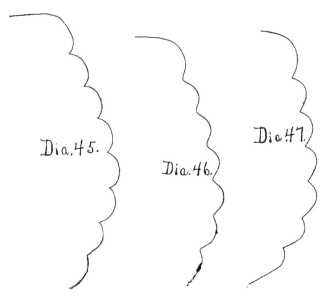

DIAGRAMS 45, 46, 47.

stead of a sort of round (see diagram 46 as to the difference) bottom or end of scallops. But how often are seen cases of shoes with the scallops all "saw tooth," like diagram 47, caused entirely by the closer on swinging the shoe much more rapidly on one side of the scallops than the other while the sewing machine is stitching and trimming.

There is but one remedy. Get another "closer on," for the one who has become accustomed to swing the shoe in a wrong manner rarely unlearns, and almost never learns to do it correctly. Scalloping is done too carelessly and has been done so for many years.

Provided the scallops have not been thrown all out of shape in closing on, it is an easy matter to bead, or turn

and cord the edges. This beading, done on a machine, and
the machine in good order, is an easy operation compared
to the old hand-tiring process where the work was aecom-
plished by main force, and then pounded by hammers. The
great trouble with beading machines is they are not kept
in good order. The same attention is not paid to them
that there is to the stitching machines.

CHAPTER IX.

A "side-lace" shoe is undoubtedly one of the neatest shoes ever worn by a lady, for there are no buttons or lumps of any kind showing on the sides, and on a well-shaped foot, made on a proper last, gives a splendid appearance.

Here is where the trouble comes in this shoe. The last must be very nearly correct in form, for there are no buttons to set over, and if the lacing is left open to fit the foot, and the last is not correct, the front seam is crooked, and the peculiar beauty of this shoe is lost. This is the shoe that

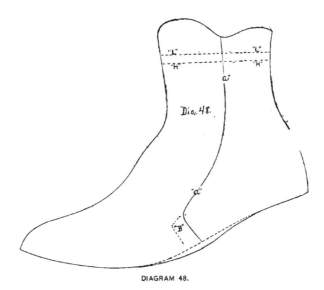

DIAGRAM 48.

shows up a bad shaped last. This is the shoe that demands a well-shaped foot. Try some of your lasts with a side-lace boot if you are at all in doubt of their being correct. It is well to try women's, misses' and children's this way to see the actual fit of the last on the foot. The side-lace never fails to show up defects back of the ball.

However, this being a nice shoe on the foot, it is a peculiar one for which to cut the pattern. If not cut right it is difficult to fit, and if cut right it is one of the easiest.

Mark around a standard, obtained as directions were given for diagram 12' and call it diagram 48. First get the large side as shown in diagram 48. Then draw the lace line, "A" "A," being particular to have it come well forward at the bottom. This will allow the shoe to go on the foot easily. Mark where the back quarter laps under the front quarter at B. Get out a quarter for front and another for back, punching stab holes at lap B as a guide for the vamper. Lay off the top of the lining position as "L," then the bottom of the facing as "H."

FRONT AND BACK QUARTERS.

In getting out the front and back quarters, add on the bottom as shown in diagram 49, front quarter, and diagram 50, back quarter, in both of which dotted lines "A" "A"

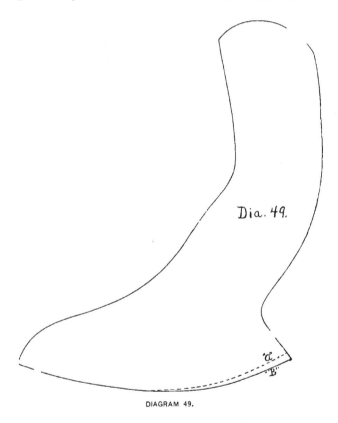

Dia. 49.

DIAGRAM 49.

show the bottom line of the large sides as taken from the standard. B B shows the addition for allowance for the in-side shank to make it last easier. The allowance is also shown in diagram 48 at bottom.

Next, mark around diagram 48 from L to L to get lin-ing, and add one-eighth of an inch all around the bottom; in the shank put a little more (see diagram 51) and take off if for McKay or welt for counter as B. Put on front quar-ter (diagram 49) evenly all around front and toe, and mark round the back of it, which leaves dotted line "C," after

which cut out a piece from the lining three-sixteenths each
way from dotted line "C." See line "D D."

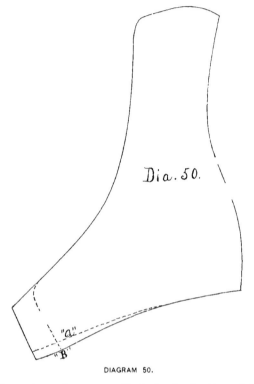

Dia. 50.

"a"

"B"

DIAGRAM 50.

One piece of pattern will do for both sides of the linings for the shoe, as one is cut without the hole, and the

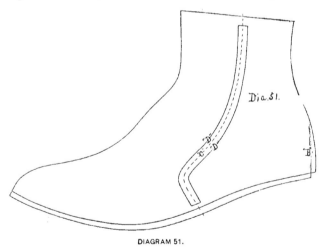

Dia. 51.

DIAGRAM 51.

other with. Next get side facing, which is so simple an operation that diagram 52 only need be shown.

In fitting place it on the lining with the hole in the centre line in the centre and stitch it on as shown in diagram.

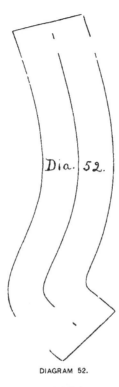

Dia. 52.

DIAGRAM 52.

53. Close the two linings (drill) back and front, after which with a pair of scissors cut the top and bottom open at H

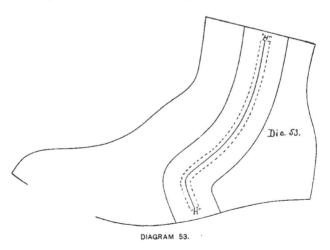

Dia. 53.

DIAGRAM 53.

when the linings are ready for the top facings. To get the top facing mark around standard diagram 48 from H to H,

which is shown by lines "A A" on diagram 54, pointing off
at "H H," diagram 48, for width of facing.   Then from
one-sixteenth of an inch at top. B B, diagram 54, cut under
until at the bottoms, "C C," it is one-fourth of an inch,
which will fit the lining seams at the front and back.   Use
front and back quarters to get the ends D E, as shown in
diagram 53.

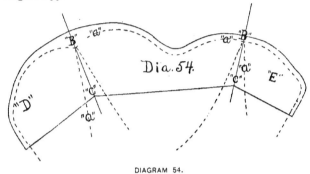

DIAGRAM 54.

Then stitch the top facing on the lining, after which
the lining is closed on by the edges of the outside, commencing at the bottom of the side stay at one side, and so
keep up stitching till clear around the upper.

"CLIMAX" BUTTON BOOT.

Next take a very peculiar button boot.   Commence
by marking around standard, diagram 12, and down the
front of the quarter, so that the same vamp may fit, using

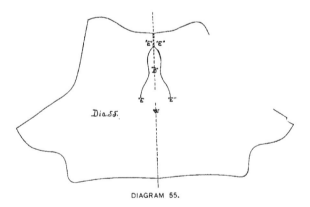

DIAGRAM 55.

the same lining patterns as well as trimming patterns.
This boot, known as the "Climax," is generally cut from
heavy stock, such as grain leather.   The vamp is used
plain,—not beaded.   This gives the quarter by drawing a
straight line as indicated by dotted line "A."   Fold the paper and cut out the quarters, as illustrated in diagram 55.

with folded line dotted at "A." While the paper is folded, cut at "B," shown as gore, in diagram 56.

If the shoe is not a familiar one it may be better understood by placing diagram 55 on standard diagram 12 and then placing the gore piece, diagram 56, folded where it is

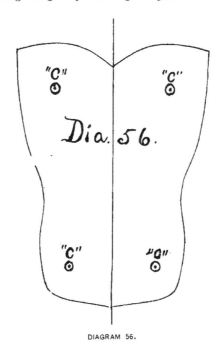

DIAGRAM 56.

shown on diagram 12. The stab holes, C C C C, diagram 56, are to be pierced so that in fitting they are placed to ooints E E E E, diagram 55, as the correct spring is so given to gore diagram 56. After getting the outside fitted, close the lining on, and complete as any button boot.

CHAPTER X.

Next take a woman's leather congress. Mark around standard, diagram 12, and get outline, after which mark gore, as illustrated in diagram 57. Also line "A" where the shoe is divided into front and back quarters, "B," "C." Of course common sense would teach that the lower the bottom of the goring, the easier the shoe will go on the foot, but again, if it is too low the shoe will yield at that point when being worn.

However, we will dissect the standard and get front quarter, diagram 58. Dotted line "A" shows the allow-

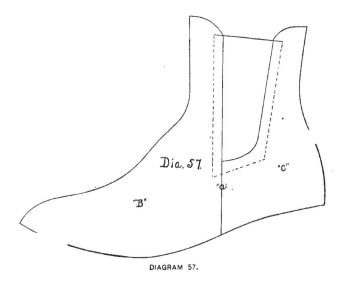

DIAGRAM 57.

ance for folding, three-sixteenths of an inch. It may be beaded on top if desired.

Diagram 59 shows the back quarter and the lap is shown at B, dotted line, while dotted line "C" shows the folded edge. In getting out a congress of any kind, width of goring must be one of the first considerations, (diagram 60), for after laying off the bottom of the goring, the height of top of shoe is governed more or less by the width of gore to be used.

This congress is simple. One can see that to make it in cloth, or serge, it is only necessary to add the difference in seams. The linings can almost be cut from the outsides, but would come a little short on the bottom and would be

full on the heel where the counter comes.   Diagram 60
shows the gore.

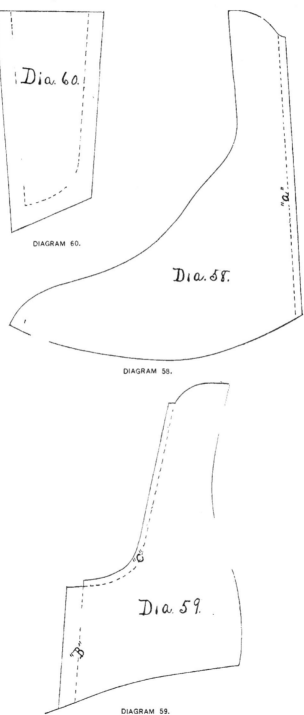

DIAGRAM 60.

DIAGRAM 58.

DIAGRAM 59.

CHAPTER XI

BUTTON BOOT WITH ROLLED TOP.

To illustrate a button boot, with a straight top rolled over inside. See diagram 61.

Mark around a standard, say in this instance diagram 12, as will be seen by the lines. Dotted line A A, is the top of diagram 12.

To make a roll top, it will, of course, be necessary to allow about one-fourth of an inch higher, as the shoe to be finished will need to be 6 inches high at the back, finished, from the vamp up, to look well. Add to line B B, cutting off diagonally at "C C"; that part is to roll over inside, consequently it should not be so long.

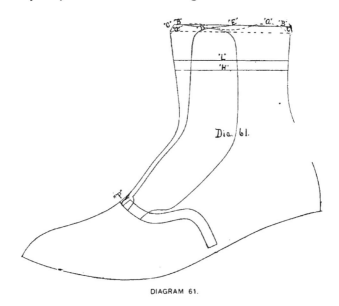

DIAGRAM 61.

Roll the top from nothing at the corner of the small quarter at D, diagram 61, until it gradually turns about three-sixteens of an inch at E, (diagrams 61 and 62), and then make an even roll until reaching the button fly at "A," diagram 61, gradually running to an even bead at B, as shown in diagram 62.

This method also allows an even bead up the front of the small quarter, as illustrated in diagram 63, until reaching "A"; when it reaches B, diagram 63, it is full roll. This method is adopted because the lining can be closed on to the outside at one continuous operation of stitching.

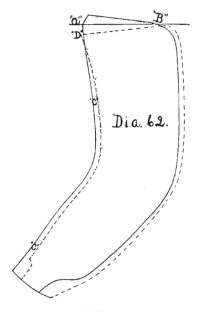

DIAGRAM 62.

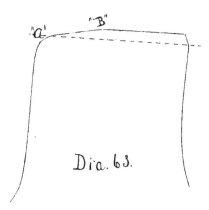

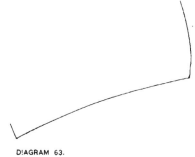

DIAGRAM 63.

Therefore the "closing on" will be no more expensive than
the regular evenly beaded shoe. After being closed on the
work of beading is no more than a regular even bead; but
the beader can do a much better job at this shoe if she will
work with the linings toward her, for then she can see how
the beading is being done.

By referring to diagram 61, it is easy to follow the line
of rolling on the whole or large quarter, then on the small
quarter, and on the button fly.

It will be noticed at P, diagram 61, that the end of the
large quarter and fly lining to match, are dropped, or slightly

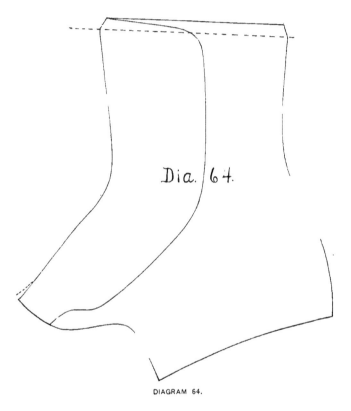

DIAGRAM 64.

cut under. This is where they go under the vamp, and it will
be found that there is plenty of stock still remaining.
Springing the fly, if one chooses, may be done. It will certainly cut as cheaply by straightening that way, and no ob-
jections to it appear, except it may cause more wrinkles
at the throat of the shoe. Diagram 64 will show very clearly the respective tops of large quarter and fly as to roll top.

Referring again to diagram 62, the heavy line all
round is the button fly proper, while the dotted line is the
fly lining, setting back on the cloth lining in front at C C,
and coming out flush with the top face lining at D.

While on this point it is proper to say that it is preferable to use a solid sheep, or napa, fly lining, on roll tops, though of course by educating the help one can get results in most unexpected cases. At a large factory making women's shoes a specialty in the State of Maine all kinds of shaped tops on button boots are rolled successfully, even where one would suppose it was practically impossible. But the foreman of the fitting room was a man who did not know the word "can't" in his department. He simply insisted on good work and finally his help had become experts at roll tops. They make a very neat finish.

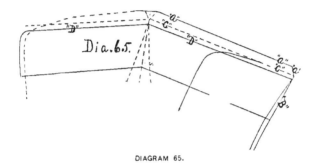

DIAGRAM 65.

Referring again to diagram 61, see at L and H, where the lines are drawn. This gives the height of or top edge of the lining and the bottom of the facing, obtained by marking round the standard and diagram 61. Recollect that the top of the outside rolls down so the top facing will be cut three-eighths of an inch narrower than it shows drawn round the top of standard diagram 61, one-fourth of an inch for allowance and one-eighth of an inch for allowance to where it is seamed on quarter.

The top of standard as shown on diagram 65 is marked A A A A, and the front B. The fold of top is dotted line "C C." The top of facing is D D.

CHAPTER XII.

Front lace shoes come next and of course it is best to take a dongola McKay, say a 4 C. Mark around standard, diagram 12, which will give the lines of a button boot. Then starting at the back of the vamp, as shown in diagram 66, begin to cut away the front, so that it may be open slightly when lasted, and when it is first put on the foot, since it must be made to accommodate the foot with a low instep, as well as to fit a high instep, by leaving it more or less open at the lacing. The shoe will also stretch after wearing a few times so it will draw closer together at the

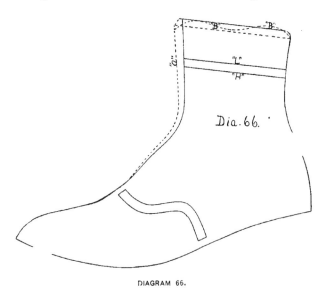

DIAGRAM 66.

lacing; but the amount to cut away must be determined by pattern cutter. There are various opinions and no fixed rule can be given. Attention is directed to the fact that it is cut away on the quarters gradually from the back of the vamp up to the top. Often the fitter who laces them together with cord of some kind, previous to their being lasted, draws them so closely together that they cannot separate sufficiently while being lasted, to find their normal condition. Thus fastened a shoe cannot be properly lasted. The laster is then held responsible, where the whole trouble is in lacing. Shoes coming to the laster with the buttons on correctly, or laced correctly, are a pleasure to last, provided the pattern is cut right. It is asking too much of the laster to try to remedy a fault caused by some one who handles the shoe before it reaches him. There would be less trouble between the lasters and their employers if these

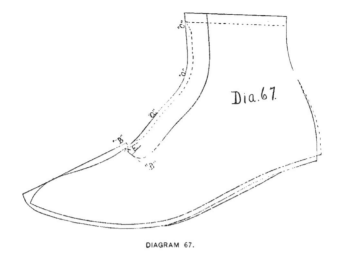

DIAGRAM 67.

two faults, unnecessary themselves, were avoided, and they could be avoided entirely by proper attention to those two important points.

Dotted line "A," diagram 66, shows the front line of button boot, and line L shows top edge of lining, while H

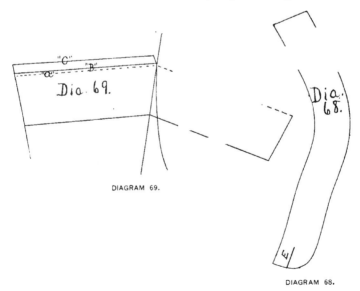

DIAGRAM 69.

DIAGRAM 68.

shows bottom of top facing. The dotted line B shows the curve top of standard button boot. This lace we will make roll top and also straight top. For the lining, see diagram

67, and so far as the bottom and back line are considered, they resemble the lines of the lining of the button boot. In front the line "A" shows the front edge of the front facing, which is the same line as the front of standard diagram 66. However, observe it is cut away about one-eighth of an inch from near the bottom end of the quarter at B until near the top, C, so the lining will not have to be cut away with the hand shears after the front facing is stitched on. There are two guides, one at the top and the other at the bottom, to place the front facing correctly. The toe seam runs about one-eighth of an inch above the end of

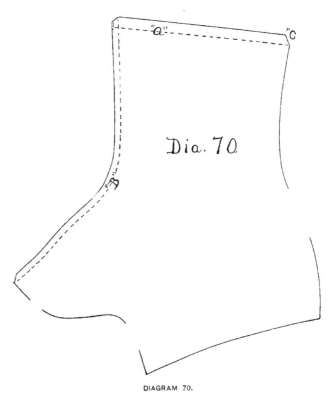

DIAGRAM 70.

the quarter. Notice the slit, E, at the lower end of the front facing, see diagram 68. In stitching the front facing on the lining the stitch should run off at E and the part marked X not stitched through but left loose. This will enable the operator to "close on" the shoe, and the vamper to throw back the lining without the necessity of its going to the "table girl" to be cut in with the hand shears, and is a neater and less expensive way The linings are closed at the back ready for the top facing. See diagram 69, in which dotted line "A" shows the top of facing line; "B" shows where the quarter is folded and line

"C" shows the top line of quarter. It is best to allow a little extra on the front end so it will not run short. After closing the quarters on either a button boot or lace that rolls inside at the top, be sure and stop off the cloth stay on the double needle machine some three-eighths of an inch from the top, or it will make a bunch where it is turned over. When staying all roll top work, the operator should commence at the bottom of the quarters, as it is easy to cut it off near the top. To get out the quarter to be folded down the front, see diagram 70, the dotted line "A" representing the fold, where it is to

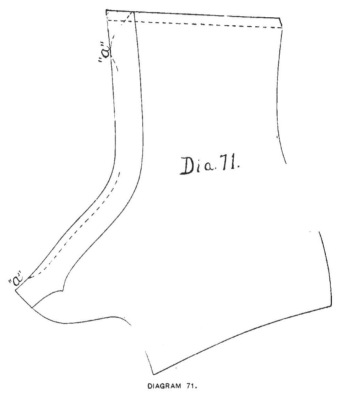

DIAGRAM 71.

roll over, and dotted line B the front line to where it will be finished after the front folding is done. Care should be taken to first close up to the corner "C" and then swing so as to follow the break at that point, as the quarters should be closed clear to the edge, but on a line with the outside. This quarter is not cut for an outside stay or facing, but the one in diagram 71 is a duplicate of diagram 70, except it has no fold in front. After leaving guides A A by which to place front facing on correctly, it is cut away so as to reduce the thickness in front, instead of cutting the quarter full down the front edge and then putting on the

facing by the edge all the way down and having
a "table girl" cut this away with hand shears. It
is best not to use a trimming knife on the machine for this purpose, as it allows the operator
to cut away material which is needed. The cutting
of it away in the pattern saves hand labor, as a cutter
will cut just as many quarters in an hour this way as he will

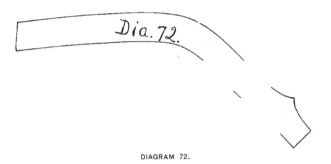

DIAGRAM 72.

in the full pattern, and then the surplus stock instead of being on the floor, where the table girl has cut it off, is in the
skin to be cut into something else. Diagram 72 shows the
facing cut so as to be plain edge. If fold is wanted simply
add it, and then fold the edge before putting the facing on
the quarter.

CHAPTER XIII.

CLOTH QUARTERS AND WELT SHOES.

Diagram 73 represents a cloth quarter cut for a foxing, and on it is shown a patent leather front facing with the fold on. Of course this facing should be folded before being placed in its present position. Dotted line "A" represents the front of the cloth quarter as well as dotted line A A all around. Dotted line "B" represents the front of fold on facing before it is folded. Line "C" is the front of

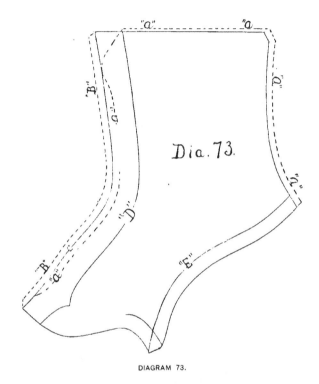

Dia. 73.

DIAGRAM 73.

facing when finished. Line "D" is back of facing. Line E at the bottom shows where the foxing edge will be.

After closing on the top it goes to the beader. Steady, or non-movable, iron or fingers or no irons are far better than vibrating ones for all straight work. After an operator becomes accustomed to it, she can do more and better work on a flat anvil with no irons for turning, for she can roll the necessary amount by manipulating the outside or lining with her fingers. Turning irons are suitable where punching out is required, and on crooked work, but they are of no use on straight work. Do not use any cement or paste or other adhesive substance in turning or beading. Simply turn, and the gauge for amount of roll is given by trying the curves of the front facings where they are to be stitched to the outside. Do not allow the operators to cement the outside quarters to the linings along the front stav, or facing. Use no cement, paste or glue here. The operator who stitches the outside to the facing can hold them correctly at no extra expense or trouble, and if the patterns are cut correctly, there is no use of "fitting" them by "table girls." That expense will thus be saved, and the shoe is not hardened at that place. If the shoe has no beaded front, the trimming knife can be used up the fronts when closing on, but if it be folded, or have a folded outside facing on, it must be stitched and the lining front

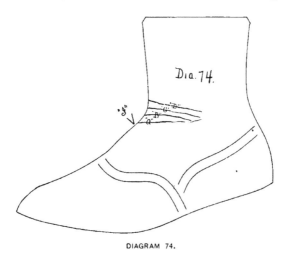

DIAGRAM 74.

facing be left extended a little, and afterwards sheared off.

In women's shoes where too soft material for inside front facings is used, there is no way except to let the shoes go to table girls, who trim out the inside facing with hand shears. The shoe is now ready to be vamped after the eyelets are put in.

By cutting the patterns according to this direction, it will be found, when you come to vamping, that the lining is ready to be thrown back and no hand shear work. After vamping close the toe seam of the linings in a lap seam, and then stitch (on the machine) across the lower end of the tongue, a little below the end of the quarters. This serves to reduce the lump at the point of juncture of so many thicknesses. Then tack clear through both quarters and the tongue, which will hold the tongue in proper position, while the strain, if any, will come, if the tongue is pulled up, on the end of the tongue where it is stitched fast to the lining.

The getting out of a misses' shoe of any kind is so similar to woman's that it does not seem necessary to dwell upon it. Of course the ball measure of the last governs the ankle measure of button boot patterns. However, the attention of all is called to the very large heel measure often seen in misses' shoes, caused by too much and too far back, so called, instep measure of the last. It is suggested, also, that the best way to try the shape of the last from the ball back to the heel, is to make a pair of side lace shoes on the last, and then try them on a fairly well shaped foot. Notice the front seam on the foot. Attention is called to diagram 74, which was a 13-E taken from a spring heel last, in which the heavy lines A B C D represent the wrinkles so often seen in shoes worn by misses. One cause of these is that the throat curve is often made too straight. Another is the last. Mould your spring heel last carefully, and while so doing, mark the place where your last maker calls instep measuring position, of your last on your mould, and after you have obtained your standard, see if that high point in your last does not come about where "V" is in diagram 74. Rather a strange place for an instep.

WELTS.

In making welts use a McKay pattern, just as it is, except the vamp which should be about 3-16 smaller all round the outside until coming near the lap on the quarters, which should be left as McKay, since it is to fit on the McKay quarters, and the shank will require about the same as McKay. But around the outside of the vamp, if one can save 3-16 of stock, the patterns for the welt vamp will cost nothing. In getting out a pattern entirely and exclusively for "turns," make the curve at the back of the leg considerably straighter than for McKay or welt, for in second lasting a turn the heel of the last stretches out the heel of the upper, and results in a much sharper curve in back of the leg of the shoe than one puts in the pattern. A curve that may look all right to the eye when the top of the leg of the empty shoe is drawn up by the hand, will be much sharper when on the foot, for the ankle is then rounded up. If a shoe is stuffed with cotton or some similar substance clear up to the top, one can see the curve the leg will have on the foot. If too much curve be in the back, it will result in the heel of the foot working up and down, and the foot will not be crowded back in the heel of the shoe. In other words, the shoe on the foot will act somewhat on the principle of a bellows.

In such a case, the leg of the shoe is really too far forward, and carries the foot forward, leaving the heel of the foot moving up and down, thus wearing the heel of the lining and stocking out. If you examine the heel of the lining after the shoe has been worn a while, you will find it worn through. It is a good idea to cut all vamp patterns from metal, even though the rest of the set be bound, as one can then alter the vamp if it be a little too large, and it is by trifles the profit on shoes comes nowadays.

CHAPTER XIV.

Next take a McKay, dongola oxford, circular vamp,
roll, or dropped top. First get a standard the same as for
button boots. Mould the last carefully, though in low

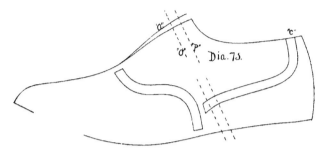

DIAGRAM 75.

cuts it is not necessary to pay attention to the height of
the heel, as in high shoes, or boots. A floor line is not
necessary.

After having got the low cut standard, next cut under
on the front to allow the shoe to be open for lacing, or
drawing the lacing. See diagram 75.

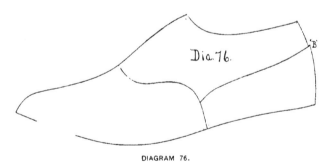

DIAGRAM 76.

Next lay off the vamp line. Then, allowing lap, lay off
the front of the quarter. If a foxed shoe is desired lay
off the top of the foxing, then, allowing lap, lay off the bottom of the quarter. It seems advisable to end a foxing,
if possible, at the top of the back of the shoe as shown in
diagram 75, "C," to prevent a lump, which is always caused
by ending it, as seen at "B," in diagram 76.

If it be a whole or seamless vamp, it is generally best

that it be finished as seen at "C," diagram 75. Reference to diagram 77 will show how the foxing is got out from the standard, diagram 75. The dotted line "A" on diagram 77 represents the stock allowed for folding, as this is to be a beaded foxing.

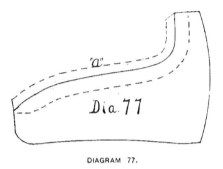

DIAGRAM 77.

WHOLE QUARTERS.

Diagram 78 shows a whole quarter got out from the same standard with the allowance for beading or folding on in front. Diagram 79 shows the fox quarter. Notice points "A" "B," where the stock of the quarter is cut away to prevent a double thickness. It also serves as a guide to assist the operator in stitching it on. At the front the outside lacing facing will be seen with the allowance for

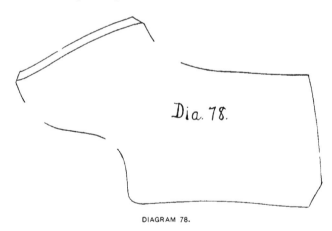

DIAGRAM 78.

folding on it. "C C" shows the line of the quarter cut away so as to save stock in cutting, and save all hand shearing. It will give two positive guides D, E, for the operator to place the facing in the right position; also a guide will be noticed at "H."

Some foremen or forewomen insist that it is necessary to cement the outside stay to the quarter after the front edge has been folded, to assist the operator in stitching it.

It would not seem necessary, if these guides are given for holding it on.

The style of the stay may be changed as desired, but the fronts of all should fit where the guides are. Slow

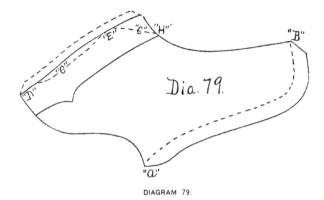

DIAGRAM 79.

down your folding machine if it runs so rapidly that the operator cannot guide sufficiently fast for it, but feld facings on the machine. Always have the folder in good order.

Next get out vamp, diagram 80, which is a duplicate

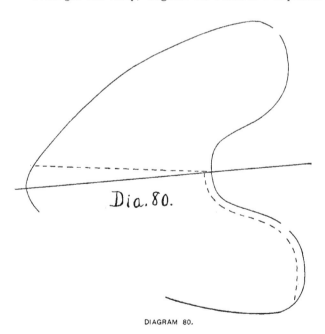

DIAGRAM 80.

of the vamp obtained for a button boot.

A few more words about dropping the toe of the vamp. Drop it when the stock is soft, and the shoe or boot is held by any method on the instep when being lasted. But one must decide such matters for himself by results obtained in each individual factory.

Diagram 81 shows the foxed quarter with the fold on in front.—Referring to diagram 75 notice straight lines "O" "P." These represent the ending of the leather quarter lining at "O" and the back of the cloth toe lining at "P."

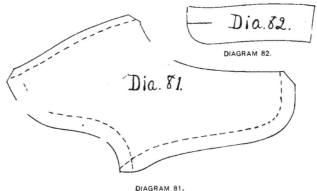

DIAGRAM 82.

DIAGRAM 81.

This is the cheap way to line the oxford, and of course there is an inside lacing facing on the cloth lining as may be seen in diagram 82, which is the facing, and diagram 83, in which may be seen the cloth lining with the facing attached. "A" represents the line of facing as finished, while "B" represents the line of the standard; "E" is the point end of

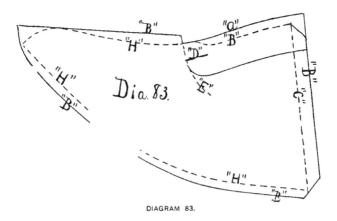

DIAGRAM 83.

the quarter as got from the standard, "D" is where the front lacing is cut in to throw back the lining without any hand shearing or table work. There should be no cement or glue used on the lining anywhere. There is no use for any.

Diagram 84 shows the quarter lining and it is got from the quarter by marking around, which gives dotted line

"A." Now as the outside quarter is to be turned over about three-sixteenths in fitting, of course it will require so much less at the top of the lining. Drop down and ahead about three-sixteenths, as shown on line "B" on top and dotted line "C" at back; then cut under at "D" for counter for McKay sewed. A lining for turn work should be cut differently. Diagram 85 will show the dotted line

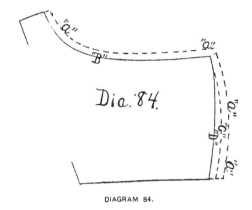

DIAGRAM 84.

"A," the line of the standard, and down the front line "B" is the line of the front of the quarter.

This line may be cut in any form, for instance, as dotted line "C" shows, but, of course, in such a case the back of the cloth lining must be made to correspond.

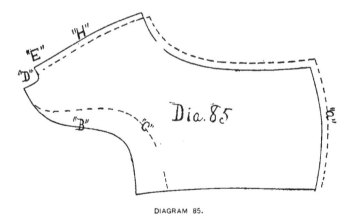

DIAGRAM 85.

The corner cut out at "D" is for the purpose of allowing the lining to be thrown back without any hand shearing, or table work, as the end of the lining quarter at "E" comes to where it is vamped. This also takes out the lump that would be there if the quarter was beaded clear down and under the vamp. It is best to add along the front edge

of the quarter lining, about one-eighth inch, so as to let it
project from the front of the outside quarter to trim away
afterwards. If it be a beaded facing on the outside, or a
beaded quarter, the only practical way to trim out the lining
is with hand shears, for the stock used in the quarter lining
is too soft to allow a trimmer to be used successfully. If it
be a plain edge quarter, then, of course, it can be trimmed
off in "closing on" by the machine.

Diagram 86 shows the cloth lining and standard mark
will be seen in the dotted line.

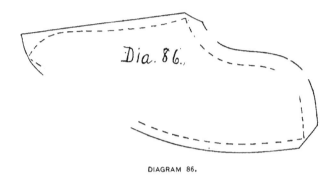

DIAGRAM 86.

To fit the shoe with the least trouble (a) close the quarters and stay them, stopping off the stay three-eighths inch
from the top; (b) close the heel seam of the quarter linings;
(c) stitch the cloth linings to the quarter linings; (d) close
around the top of the quarters on to the quarter linings;
(e) roll the top on a beading machine, using no turning
fingers; (f) stitch all round, and down the front; then eyelet,
vamp and close the toe seam of lining. Stitch the tongue
to the cloth lining three-eighths inch ahead of the end of
the quarter, to prevent so much of a lump at vamping point,
tacking through the quarters and tongue.

CHAPTER XV

To make an even bead oxford, round the corner of the quarter, so the operator may close the outside on the lining at one operation, and allow on the top of the quarter lining about one-twelfth inch, so the operator can close on with a trimming knife. Before the oxfords are lasted they

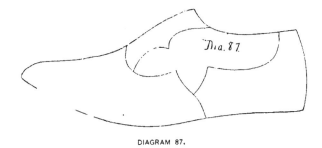

DIAGRAM 87.

should be laced slightly open. Probably the best way to do that, having all open alike, is to provide a wedge-shaped piece of iron or wood fastened to the lacer's bench, and when lacing the shoes lace around the wedge.

Diagram 87 shows a neat oxford to fit the same linings.

Diagram 88 shows another which cuts very cheaply. It is called a plug circular vamp. Use the same linings as in

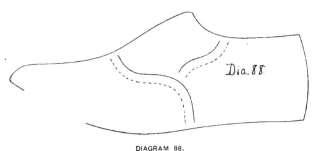

DIAGRAM 88.

preceding styles. It is just as well to have but one set of linings for all oxfords to be used on the same last, provided they are all the same outline.

Diagram 89 shows another style of oxford, obtained by marking around and through standard diagram 75, at line of curve of vamp as at diagram 89 "B," so that one may use the same set of lining patterns.

In cutting this style, (diagram 89), you are referred to diagram 90, for half vamp. If the paper be folded on line "A," (diagram 90), it will give a whole vamp. In this the

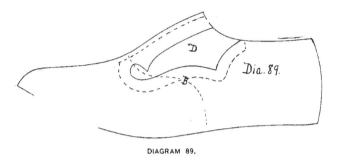

DIAGRAM 89.

lacing facing cuts very cheaply, and by putting a piece of leather or cloth in the vacancy, "D," (diagram 89) it makes a very nice style. The piece of insertion should be cut as diagram 91 and as dotted line "A" shows the edge of the

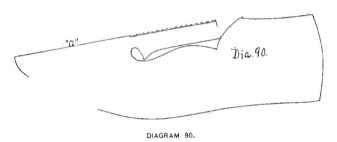

DIAGRAM 90.

facing. In diagram 91, it is cut under about one-eighth inch to prevent too much thickness at lacing edge. In diagram 89, the inserted piece is shown all round by dotted lines.

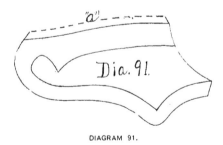

DIAGRAM 91.

To get the facing in diagram 89 spring up just enough. Cut a pattern from the hole "D," as shown in diagram 92, using it as a guide in fitting.

CHAPTER XVI.

NEWPORTS, SOUTHERN TIES, AND LOW CUTS.

Diagram 130 represents a low cut. It represents the instep in its correct position without being forced down by a tight lacing or buttoned too hard. The gore is shown by "A." There is no lacing to this shoe. It can be adapted to men's wear, or children's shoes, and is easy on the foot. The vamp is cut whole, being folded on line "B," which

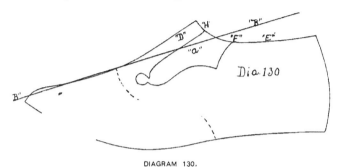

DIAGRAM 130.

throws the tongue "D" down into the gore instead of being sprung up in fitting.

Diagram 131 shows the gore piece, and should be whipped together at "A" by hand. Use only a few stitches so as to hold in position while being fitted. Just draw the edges at "A" together and it will give a curved line up the front if the gores are cut with a curve at that point. The draught of the gore is in the right direction to make the shoe fit well. If a congress could only be cut so that the

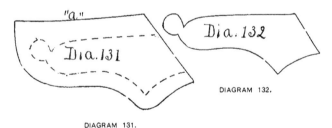

DIAGRAM 131.

DIAGRAM 132.

gore, instead of simply drawing hard across the ankle, would draw from instep to heel, an easier fitting shoe could be obtained, beside the leg would be gently forced back, and the heel would not get so far forward. The wrinkles which show so badly just above the vamp at the back would not be there.

Diagram 132 shows a pattern used to mark the gore so as to fit correctly.

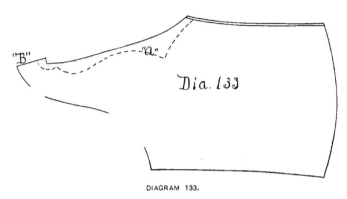

DIAGRAM 133.

Diagram 133 shows the quarter lining cut from sheep, and at "A" the dotted line shows the line of the opening of the vamp.

Diagram 134 shows the sheep tongue lining, dotted line A showing the edge of the centre piece.

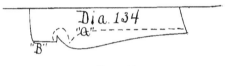

DIAGRAM 134.

Diagram 135 shows one-half of the drill vamp lining, it being cut folded at "A." In getting out the patterns for this shoe three-sixteenths inch should be added at "E," diagram 130, to fold before it is fitted. The first operation will be to fold at "E," then to put gores in where they belong, using cement or glue, and taking diagram 132 to

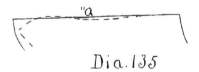

DIAGRAM 135.

mark the gores. After letting the cement set, stitch around the gore close to the edge of the leather from F to H (diagram 130), one row. Next close tongue lining to quarter lining at B (diagrams 133 and 134), and this should be a closed and rubbed seam. Next stitch vamp lining to the quarter lining and tongue lining. Then close the heel seams of vamp, and lining, after which place the lining inside the vamp and stitch a row all round until you reach the gores. The second row of stitching will fasten the lining in. Then trim off the surplus lining on the top.

In lasting this shoe care and judgment must be exercised. Since the front or instep line is cut under the line

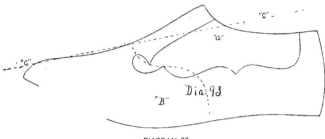

DIAGRAM 93.

of the last to allow the gore to draw sufficiently on the foot, the laster may draw it down some in the shank, but not too much. Some foremen think it best in making any gored shoe to stitch in one or two pieces of drill or webbing from one side of the gore to the other so as to prevent the strain in lasting coming wholly on the gore. When the shoe comes off the last trim out the pieces with hand shears.

Diagram 93 shows another style obtained from same outline. "A" represents cloth. Dotted line "C" is line to fold. "B" is the leather vamp. Of course the edges of the

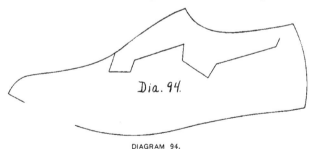

DIAGRAM 94.

facing and the fancy cut edges will be raw, as there is no stock to fold, but they may be thinned down.

Diagram 94 shows a cut for oxfords called "Electric." This can be folded on the edge where the insertion or plug goes.

Diagram 95 shows a "Newport button" or button oxford. The general idea of design is balanced all through, and the cutting and fitting exactly the same as an ordin-

ary button boot; in fact it is only the lower part of a button boot.

Diagram 96 is a "Southern tie" and a very popular
shoe (1897) on the Pacific coast. This is rather a peculiar

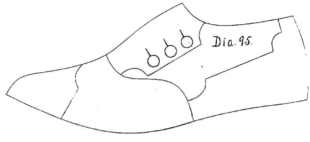

DIAGRAM 95.

shoe to fit, and yet easy if the pattern is cut correctly, and
no table work. You will notice that all the propositions
unusual in pattern cutting, advised in this work are for the
purpose of obviating the uncalled-for "table fitting," or as

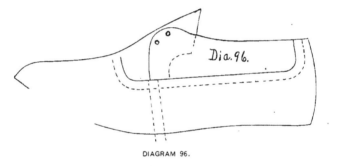

DIAGRAM 96.

it is sometimes called "pasting," formerly considered as
necessary as sewing machines.

The beading on this shoe where the lining is stitched
on must of necessity be what is termed "even cord," as the

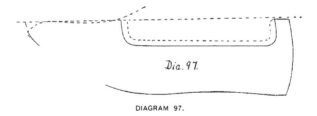

DIAGRAM 97.

ear, where the eyelet holes are, will not admit of roll. Their
shape precludes such a result. The standard, diagram 96,
is got as usual from the last, after which lay out vamp line
and lap; then the tongue and quarter. The back of the
tongue must not be too far to the rear, or the shoe will be

difficult to get on the foot. The outline of the vamp is shown on diagram 97.

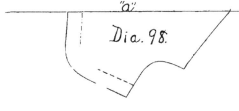

DIAGRAM 98.

Diagram 98 shows one-half the tongue as obtained from the standard, the line being the fold. This is for a tongue with no seam in it. Where a seam up the front is desired, better lines can be secured by cutting the front to the curves desired.

DIAGRAM 99.

When lasting a whole "tongue southern tie," have the laster put a little paste in between the outside and lining of the tongue, as it then dries to the shape of the last, and holds its curves better.

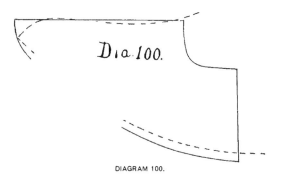

DIAGRAM 100.

Diagram 99 shows the quarter with the vamp lines dotted.

Diagram 100 shows one-half the vamp lining cut for the drill, and the standard in dotted lines shows how to get the vamp.

Diagram 101 shows the quarter lining cut in such a manner as not to vamp through, leaving plenty of room for the counter. The margin to close on by will be seen around the top. It is cut in at "A" for the purpose of allowing the tongue to be fitted in.

In this place it is preferable to stitch the tongue lining on to the vamp lining first. Stitch the tongue lining on to

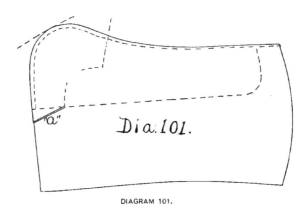

DIAGRAM 101.

the tongue, the tongue to the front of the vamp, care being taken not to stitch through the vamp lining. Stitch the quarters on to the quarter lining down to the slit "A," diagram 101. Bead the quarters, stitch the vamp on, leaving the lining loose, then stitch the vamp lining to the quarter lining from "A," diagram 101, down to the bottom.

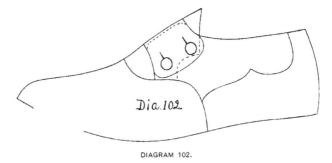

DIAGRAM 102.

Diagram 102 is a "Southern button." It is about the same fitting as the "Southern tie," except the shoe requiring two quarters, as one must be long enough to fold so as to make the button fly, and the other is short, only taking the buttons. It being a circular vamp makes it cut cheaper.

CHAPTER XVII.

STRAP SANDALS AND OPERA SLIPPERS.

A one "Strap Sandal" has been a very favorite shoe in Canada, and most Canadian ladies who wear low cut shoes seem to prefer this to any other. A good deal depends on the last this shoe is made on as to its fit on the foot. An Oxford last is not the correct one.

A last to make a good fitting strap sandal should be inclined toward the "rocker bottom," and especially so at the toe; while for "opera" slippers, a real "rocker bottom" last is required, though with proper judgment some spring in the shank may be used. One of the points in fitting a sandal is the "binding." There have been improvements in the mechanism for binding, and the crude way in which it was formerly done, by stitching it fast on one edge, then turning it over and stitching the other down, is out of date .

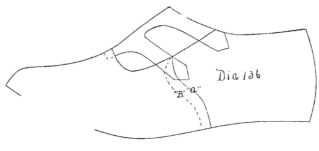

DIAGRAM 136.

An "English binder" on a cylinder sewing machine with a feed at both top and bottom, does the work well. The work moves along very nicely and gives good results. However, a good operator is quite an assistance. The binding should fit the binder very accurately, and it will be necessary to see that the needle sews a little closer on the outside edge than on the under side of the binding.

Another part of fitting on sandals is putting in the lining. Some fitters paste the lining in nearly edge to edge, then trim out the lining to the edge of the outside with hand shears. It is usually better to stitch the lining to the outside with a coarse stitch, using a trimming knife on the machine before binding. Some factories cut the lining by the outside. When the strap is pieced this brings the seam of the piece in the same place both in the lining and outside. But if the strap is made with the seam in a different place it reduces the lump at that point. In lasting a sandal, or in fact any low cut shoe that is not held at the instep by lacing, buttons or some other way, it is wrong to pull with the pincers in the shank, or behind the ball of the last, as such a shoe can be drawn out of shape in such a manner. It is difficult to make a really first class line of button boots and low cuts, and have them lasted by the same lasters. Also if making strap sandals, or sandals of any kind, they should not have the buttons put on until they are finished, for, if

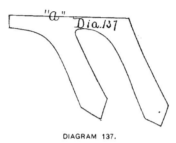

DIAGRAM 137.

put on before, the laster is liable to button the strap and try to make it hug the instep.

Diagram 136 shows a two strap sandal.

Just cut a whole vamp, and afterwards cut it pieced, as at "A"-"B." The strap, one-half, is cut separate (see diagram 137) and folded at line "A." Diagram 136 shows where it is stitched on the vamp. This makes a very neat and cheap slipper, the straps being fastened with buttons on the sides. It is generally bound on the edges.

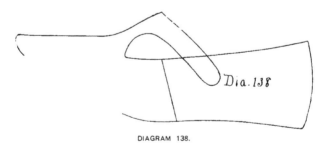

DIAGRAM 138.

Another sandal is shown at diagram 138. It is an-other cheap cutter as compared with its finished appear-ance. Referring to diagram 139 it will be seen how cheaply the vamp cuts.

A good many vampers have used a drill lining in the top of button and lace boots, sometimes using a fancy stitch across it where the bottom of the facing would come if one were used. But it is rare such a lining is seen without bad wrinkles, especially down the back curve. Diagram 140 illustrates the manner in which to get out the linings which run to the top and no facing to prevent wrinkles. It is all in the little outward sweeps at the top as seen at "B B." "D D" represents the lines of the outside quarters, and A A the seams taken in the linings (supposed to be one-fourth inch). It will be seen by reference to the diagram that this swell at the top of the linings makes the seams of the quarters at the tops fit perfectly the seams of the linings. The idea is

DIAGRAM 139.

that the tops of the linings must be large enough so that the lining seams and the seams of the outside quarters match each other, while just below there the linings must be small enough to fit inside smoothly. This does it. It is sometimes preferable to cut the tops of the cloth linings straight across from the two highest points, as it is easier for the lining cutter. They are closed on with a trimming knife so it costs nothing to cut it out. All sewing machine

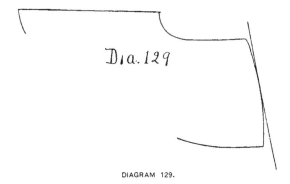

DIAGRAM 129.

companies now have a wide throat plate—used in closing on with a knife—so as to leave a wide extension of cloth outside of the stitch to prevent it fraying out.

Of the work on women's opera slippers, reference to the last having already been made, it is necessary to only look at the one peculiarity of the cut of the upper, as illus·

trated in diagram 129. It is shown with a straight cut
seam with the full line, while the curved line shows the
proper way to cut it. As may be readily seen, if this side is
closed and stayed, as the back of a button boot, it will result
in the top and bottom edge being reduced in length, while
the centre will bulge, and show a fullness. This will cause
it to hug the foot, and last under better. This upper must
not be dropped at the toe of the vamp, and should not be
touched with the pincers back of the place where the
vamp comes on top of the last. Allow three-eighths inch
for lasting in this shoe and three sizes longer than the last
for turns, all owing to conditions. Nearly all opera slippers
are more or less made turns. People unacquainted with the
methods and facilities that Haverhill, Mass., possesses would
hardly believe how cheaply turns can be produced.

CHAPTER XVIII.

Diagram 141 shows a serge congress, the quarter cut as usual. Diagram 142 shows it in an improved way to save stock.

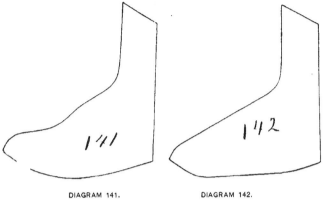

DIAGRAM 141.   DIAGRAM 142.

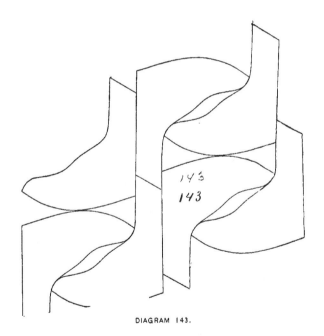

DIAGRAM 143.

Diagram 143 shows the way it is usually cut, and diagram 144 shows the saving in the new way, which will average one and one-half yards of serge saved on 60 pair cases. Of course the vamp will be somewhat straighter on the front line in a finished shoe, but the lining, being cut to the shape of the last, serves to plump it out.

The 142 cut seems to want more pulling down at the sides of the ball in lasting; but, being serge, is drawn down

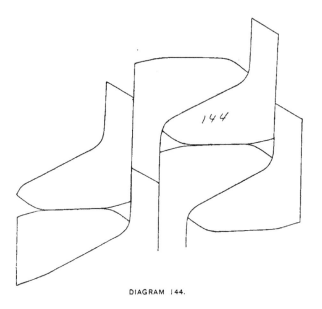

DIAGRAM 144.

very easily. In fact, it can be lasted at the sides with the fingers. A shoe from this pattern will never become squatty, as a serge congress often does. Of course, such a shoe is not expected to be very stylish.

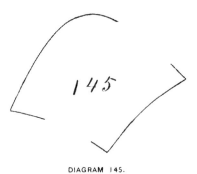

DIAGRAM 145.

The next will be an ordinary patent tip (diagram 145) cut as usual, while diagram 146 is the same tip cut to save stock and gives the same appearance in the shoe as 145.

In putting tips on shoes, it is well to have them about one-eighth inch back from the edge of the vamp all around, for then the tacks just catch and a good deal of stock saved.

DIAGRAM 146.

CHAPTER XIX

MEN'S SHOES.

In starting on a man's standard it is necessary to select a last, and of course a middle size, say a 7 or 8; also as to width, a 3 or 4 wide if the goods are to be fine, and a 5 or 6 wide if the goods are to be coarse. Begin with a fine McKay sewed button, as it will probably be best suited for a start. After having selected the last, draw the lines up the front and down the heel as central as the eye gives it. Then proceed to get a paper mould as described for getting it in women's work. After obtaining the mould mark around it, and add one-half an inch to the bottom for lasting. See diagram 100X. This one-half inch added is added on the

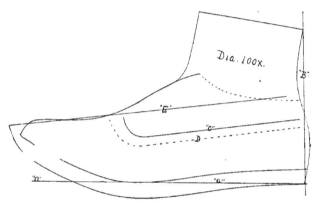

DIAGRAM 100X.

bottom of the last for stock to last over, and if very heavy stock to be used may require more. After that measure down from the mould at the heel to obtain the floor line "A." Erect a perpendicular at heel "B" one-fourth of an inch, inside the full part of the heel.

After drawing the perpendicular at the heel, measure up five and one-half to six inches from the bottom of the last for the height of the back of the leg. Generally it is best to cut the leg higher when the shoe is coarse and cheap, than when it is to be a fine shoe. The curve at the back of the leg must be put in with the eye in absence of any assistance such as prepared curves.

After getting the back curve, find out the girth of the ball of the last. Make the front of the ankle across where the back curve is sharpest the same measure as half the ball after adding sufficient for front and back seam. Then slant the top of the leg in front, back toward the heel, as the ankle will require to be larger where the ankle bone comes. When the shoe is on the foot the swell of the ankle joint as it projects takes up the leather so as to curve the back of the leg of the shoe a good deal more than it curves when the shoe is off. This prominence of ankle joint is much greater in men than in women.

Shoes made on the wider widths of lasts are generally for stout people, while the reverse applies to thin people. Consequently in getting out patterns, this should be taken into consideration.

After getting the front of the leg, to get the top some eye judgment must be used, so that the shoe will look well. Put in the throat curve, which will be much straighter, or on a larger radius than that used on women's shoes for the same reason of the lesser curve on the back of the ankle. The ankle joint pushes out the upper at the point against which it rests, acting upon the back of the ankle and the throat in such a manner as to curve it inward.

If the top of the last is too thick, it will cause a fullness just below the ankle joint, and upon standing with the weight of the body upon the foot wrinkles will be observed running lengthwise of the foot between the ankle joint and the top of the vamp. A fullness extends over the counter which will probably settle into small wrinkles after the shoe has been worn a few times.

These small points if obviated in lasts and patterns will certainly result in a shoe of better appearance both off and on the foot.

Next try the last with the size stick. Better allow four sizes more in length of pattern, until a different allowance is found necessary. A good trial or two will settle such points, and no positive allowance can be laid down, as conditions in different factories vary so.

The difference in the stock used in the vamps is great, and allowance of length must be governed entirely by what is necessary. If the factory cuts nothing but calf, or any stock with about the same amount of stretch in it, of course it is easy to determine the allowance.

If the pattern man who works for a factory, whether he be in the factory or doing the work outside, is a man of good shoe factory experience, which is necessary to success, and is also endowed by nature with a good fund of common sense, he should be allowed a good deal of latitude. He should show in results that his end of the business is loaded down with means of saving in many ways. A man who is really good on patterns, should also be really good in all his ideas of fitting shoes. He should be capable to go into the fitting room with his ideas. If he advances any new ones, whether they be original or borrowed, they should be thoroughly tried, and if found beneficial, adopted.

We have now the standard for a man's button shoe, except laying out the vamp and the lines of lap on the quarters. The length of vamp is governed entirely by ideas. In this measure off on the toe about five-eighths of an inch for lasting and then measure back four inches as length. The height of the back of vamp or golosh is also a matter of opinion in this standard.

After laying out the vamp line "C," allow one-third inch for lap, which gives the bottom of the quarter ,shown by dotted line "D"; but when reaching the front lap of vamp on the quarters, allow a little surplus stock so that when the vamp in being stitched on, if very soft, stretchy material,

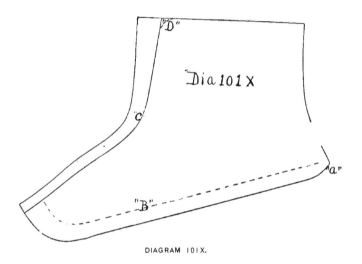

DIAGRAM 101X.

it will still find place to catch on. Then cut out the lap on standard, and round the toe of vamp up to straight fold line "E."

It is now an easy matter to get out the quarters as per diagram 101X. It is well to round off the bottom at "A," as it takes out the lump. Dotted line "B" shows the lap of vamp and line "C" shows the small quarter cut away. This is usually left a square corner at "D." The top of the quarters are stitched to the lining clear across both quarters until the fly is reached, then the upper is rolled over at the top so as to turn down inside about three-sixteenths of an inch. When stitched around the small quarter, the front is either stitched down on the lining and the cloth lining trimmed off and left raw edge, or the cloth lining is folded by hand so that the folded edge will be just right to make a smooth lining. The small quarter is sometimes then left raw edge and in other cases it has the proper allowance for folding, and is folded. This makes neat finish, but is unnecessarily expensive.

Here is illustrated a way to fit this button shoe, and yet after the help has had a little practice it gives a first class result at a much less expense.

Round the corner of the small quarter at "D," as dotted line shows. Then get out the fly from the large quarter as shown in diagram 102X, in which line "A" is exactly the front of the quarter until it reaches point on which to swing "B," when dotted line "C" the rest of the way up is the quarter.

Place the pencil on point shown at "B" and swing the quarter to get the spring in the fly, then the back of the

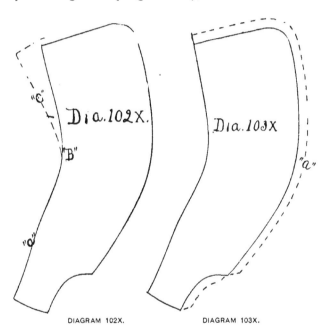

DIAGRAM 102X.   DIAGRAM 103X.

fly as laid off by the eye, generally from about half the width of the leg at the top.

If a button fly is to be plain, it is advisable to spring it some, as even the stretch it gets over the turning iron will lengthen the edge. In men's shoes it is generally folded along the edge, the edge allowance being put on the pattern and then stitched to the fly lining, allowing the edge to project a little so that it may be trimmed off closely by a Barber trimmer, if the stock be of a firm character or by hand shears if the stock be soft.

This fly is arranged to fold on the Lufkin machine all around the outside edge as will be seen by reference to diagram 103X, dotted line "A."

Use diagram 102X and add around the edge. Diagram 102X is also useful to get out the fly lining. See diagram 104X.

After folding the fly, it is best to close it on to the large quarter, leaving the top down to where the top of the quarters will be rolled when finished, but before closing the outside on to the lining, it is well to fit the button. fly lining on to the lining. It will be noticed in diagram 104X

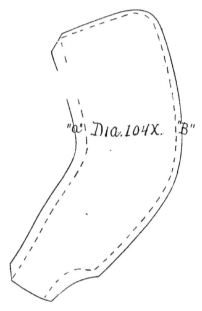

DIAGRAM 104X.

that there is left on in front at "A" one-quarter inch to fold over and make a stay by stitching through.

The margin "B" is left on, to trim off, after being closed on. Of course it is not necessary to leave the one-quarter inch on in front, if one does not care to make it answer for stay.

A man's button may also be cut to close on in same way as the straight top woman's. This reduces the expense, but some do not like it, as it leaves an even cord or bead down the side of the fly. It does very well on medium priced work, however. .

CHAPTER XX.

CONCERNING VAMPS.

Next get out a half vamp from diagram 100X, and call it diagram 105X.

This vamp as got from the standard would nearly always be too long where it is vamped to fit the quarters, caused principally by the stretch in vamping. It is usual to cut off at the heel say three-sixteenths of an inch as dot-

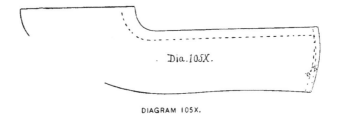

DIAGRAM 105X.

ted line "A" in diagram 105X, but some of large experience claim that it is not stretched on the bottom in fitting and does not need shortening, hence at the top cut off only at dotted line "B."

Where one uses a machine (cylinder) with a feed both under the work and the foot also feeding, the vamp will not

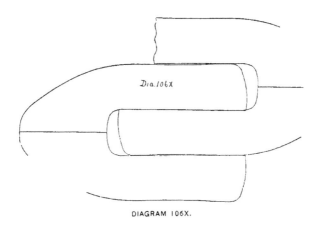

DIAGRAM 106X.

stretch so much.

Another way to prevent, in a great measure, the stretching of the vamp is to "foot line" with a piece of drill from the heel to the ball, by cementing it on the vamp while it is still flat. This serves also to prevent the vamp from

stretching so much while being lasted. Vamps cut from
calf, or any small skin, where it is necessary in getting good
vamps to keep the toe to the back bone and heels to the
flank, are sure to stretch, if not prevented in some manner.

And now about vamps being closed at the heel, or
made to interlock. If it be desired to have a shoe draw in
the very best possible manner, it is best to cut the vamp so
the fore part is about on a line with the top of the last.
This will give it just about the proper "spring," and in patent leather it is almost necessary to adhere to this plan, as
this is a shoe to be handled carefully.

In standard diagram 100X, the vamp is got out without regard to closing at the heel or interlocking. An interlocking or reversing vamp, so as to cut the heel of one into
the throat of the other, is shown in diagram 106X. Round
off the lower corner of the heel, as it sometimes saves stock
and is easier cut.

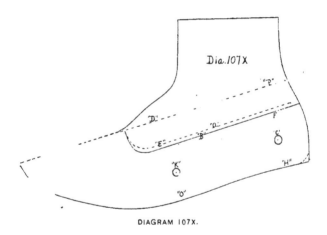

DIAGRAM 107X.

Diagram 107X shows a standard from the same last
as diagram 100X, and the same outline; but it also shows
how an interlocking vamp is got at the first effort, also
leaving the sides or wings of the vamp as high as possible
and still have them interlock.

In making it interlock, the spring of the vamp may
not be just as the last would call for it, for in this case it
is governed by the amount of opening, or throat, at the
heel.

Get the fold line of the vamp in the following way.
First, it is necessary to get the one-half throat at D, E, with
dividers. Then place one point of dividers at H, and measure twice, which gives you "F." This is the width of the
vamp at heel. See that one-half the measure from E to O
is measured up from F, by finding it at K, which gives you
the fold as shown at dotted line P. This gives the line to

fold to get half of the vamp, and if done carefully a reversing vamp that will not waste any stock in cutting will be the result.

Regarding men's vamps.—A "right and left" vamp is needed on the so-called "bull dog" of circular vamp, because the toe is so far to the inside, and the outside ball swells out so much. In factories cutting the finest shoes for which a good price is obtained, patterns are generally cut right and left. Lasts, as the majority are made, have the comb and the shanks in such positions, relative one to the other as to preclude the possibility of a perfect shoe from a straight pattern.

This may not give quite the vamp desired, but the heights at sides will be all possible to get. In wide lasts, a good vamp is got this way, and as the coarser grade of shoes are mostly made on wide lasts, the shoes come out very satisfactorily. It is said by manufacturers that it is quite a saving to have two styles of vamp patterns in cutting some stock of large spread, one to reverse, and the same vamp closed at the heel, and to have the cutter exer-

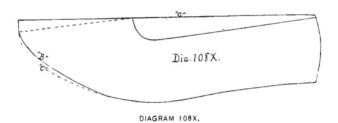

DIAGRAM 108X.

cise his judgment in cutting by using either, or that which cuts best in each case.

In practice this really saves leather. In coarse goods they are often run right together in vamping, some open and some closed heels put on the same case of shoes. Repeatedly the two shoes of one pair were made differently, one with the open vamp, the other with the closed heel. Afterwards it was impossible for any one to tell which was which, one deciding one way, and the next the contrary, and after a few days the same person in more than one instance selected the opposite from the one he had selected formerly.

To get the closed heel vamp, take the half-vamp got from diagram 107X and by marking around it as seen in diagram 108X, get the fold line "A." Then to have the toe correct mark around the toe as line "B," which will cut away the surplus as shown by dotted line "C." For a last with a very hollow shank, this spring vamp is as good as any, if the stock to be cut is fairly heavy. It gives a surplus of stock to draw into the shank.

To get out the lining for the button shoe, mark around the standard diagram 100X, which gives line "A" "A," diagram 109X, and through the vamp and quarter lap. This gives lines "B," "C." Add on all around the bottom about three-sixteenths of an inch (see line "D") and then cut away down the heel from line of vamp as seen at "E." Put on toe seam from bottom of quarter. Next take off one-fourth inch at top, as shown by line "F," for the top of the outside is to roll over. Notice line "L," which marks off the top of the lining. If a top facing is to be used, line H shows bottom of facing. When closing the outside on to the quarters let the cloth lining project above the quarters a little, to prevent fraying out; but if a top facing is to be used, close on with a small seam only.

Common sense teaches that the quarters will roll a little more with a full lining than when a facing is used. The

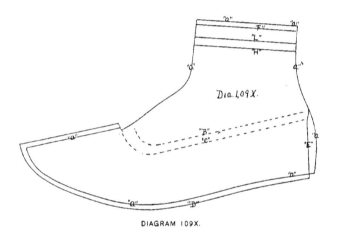

DIAGRAM 109X.

extra roll is caused by closing the quarters on a little lower on the whole lining. It is usual to stitch an inside back stay on the lining down to the vamp lining, leaving lining and stay entirely loose from vamp line to the bottom. This allows the shoe to draw to the last. Nothing will then interfere with the counter, beside it does away with the lump caused by seaming. This shoe is generally vamped through the lining with good results.

It may be, as is sometimes the case, that it will be necessary to add say one-eighth inch up along the instep on a standard when getting it out for a button shoe. This applies when a rather large seam is to be taken up the front in fitting the shoe, and when a stay is to be made of the fly lining to prevent the side of the vamp from bowing up at that point in lasting. All such trifles should at once be remedied by the pattern man.

MEN'S LACE AND CONGRESS. LASTING.

The lasting of men's shoes is a matter on which a good deal could be written.   In the first place consider hand lasting. A prevailing opinion is that a man's upper should not be back lasted. It is claimed by some that more stretch can be got out of a shoe to back last it.

The shoe should be drawn well over the toe, a tack or two driven, and the sides of the toe and the heel fastened well before the sides of the ball are lasted.   I prefer the tacks at the toe on the end of the last be drawn after the side tacks are in, and so allow the upper to be lasted along the ball without the laster having to work against the straight line of the vamp strained lengthwise.

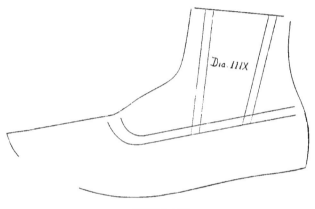

DIAGRAM IIIX.

If one wishes to use his own mixture on a patch of cloth for a box, I would recommend powdered glue in liquid acetic acid, adding rye flour until it is of the right consistency.   Oil of cloves in it is good to prevent mildew or mould.

As to lace shoes, to match the button boot just de-scribed. Mark around standard diagram 100X and through vamp and quarter line. Swing back from the end of quar-ter at the front bottom end to about five-sixteenths inch at top front, more or less if you choose.   This gives a lace standard. There is nothing special to get out for this, as we have the vamp in the button shoe, and to get out the quarter is simply to mark around the quarter in the standard.   The lining is obtained the same as in the button, except the front

line, and that is obtained from the quarter, while the front of
the lining should be cut away under the facing on the same
principle as in woman's. If a folded front is wanted on the
quarter, it is put on, and the same applies to the vamp.
Common sense cuts patterns, a natural gift gets up new de-
signs.   Rules apply in all cases if used with judgment.
There is no arbitrary set of rules for pattern makers.

The congress shoe may be taken next. First get out
a whole vamp.   Then get out a standard as for
diagram 100X; but as there is no seam to be taken
off the front of the leg, and as it is a congress, cut under
measure slightly at this point. If any other change reduce
the width at top of leg, so as to make the gore hug the
leg, and prevent any fullness at that point.

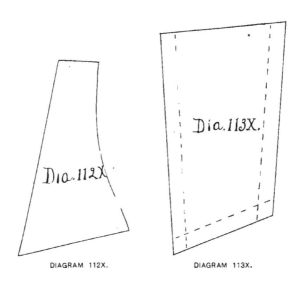

DIAGRAM 112X.   DIAGRAM 113X.

Next lay out the vamp, diagram 111X, and lap on the
quarters and gore. Measure each side of the centre of the
leg top, for the gore, making it as wide as desired.   Then
lay off the lap of gore under the quarters, after which cut
out all laps and use this standard to get the pieces. Get
out the vamp, following with the back quarter and gore,
as seen in diagram 112X and 113X.

Next we will get out the front quarter pattern which
we will use to "cut in" the quarters after they have been
crimped. See diagram 114X. This quarter we will use to
get the crimp form, which may be a wood crimp, or the iron
form used on a crimping machine. The front line should
be sharpened at the throat, or rather the front of the leg
should be thrown forward, as seen in diagram 115X, in
which the dotted line shows the front quarter cutting in

pattern, and the full line the shape to make the crimp. Different stock may work better with less or more curve in it.

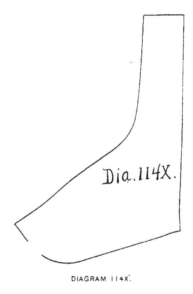

DIAGRAM 114X.

Now for blocking pattern for the front quarter, diagram 116X. Place the front of it on dotted line B, which

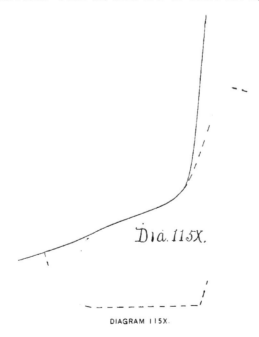

DIAGRAM 115X.

will represent the fold of a piece of paper and will be the centre line of the blocker. Mark around the bottom of the

front pattern from C to D and from D to E. Then place
the finger on the place marked A and swing the front pattern
so as to get another mark from H to K. Then place the finger on spot marked L and swing again, keeping the front
of the front quarter near line B. Mark from O to P, after
which mark across the top as at R. This gives the amount
of stock, roughly estimated, after which an allowance is
made to compare with that shown in diagram 116X.

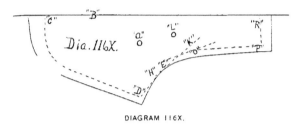

DIAGRAM 116X.

There seems to be no set rule whereby any one can get a
perfect blocker the first time, as it largely depends on the
stock to be crimped, the manner in which it is to be
crimped, whether bv machine or by hand, or on a brake.
It also depends a good deal on the man who crimps it. It
is well to use the rule laid down as far as practical, being
governed in many instances by the case in hand. Sometimes
repeated trials may be needed.

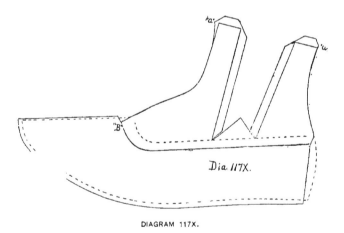

DIAGRAM 117X.

When the front quarter is crimped with the form
sharper than the cutting-in form, it is expected that the cutter will see that the crimp curve is made to match that of
the cutting in pattern by twisting or straightening the
leather.

Diagram 117X shows all parts of a whole cut lining
with edges folded around the gore so clearly that there is

scarcely any explanation needed. Get the outline from
standard diagram 111X, and only depart from the regula-

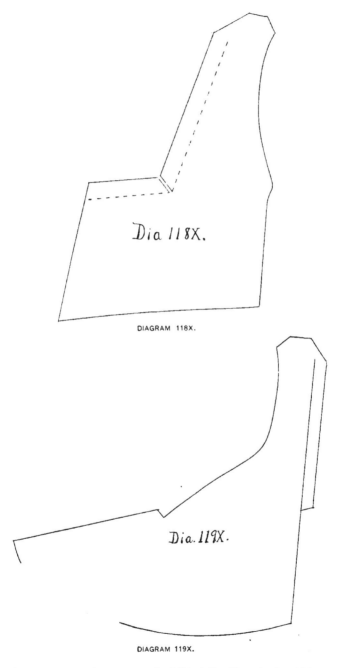

Dia 118X.

DIAGRAM 118X.

Dia. 119X.

DIAGRAM 119X.

tion pattern at the tops marked "A A." Here it should be
thrown out so as to meet the top edges of the outside.

These two little swells are essential points in making a smooth lining. The point at B is slightly cut under so as to give a surplus of lining up the instep. This will prevent the shoe from hitting too hard at that point in the lining and so preventing the outside from coming down tightly to the last, as is often seen in congress shoes.

In diagrams 118X and 119X is shown the congress lining cut in two pieces, as is sometimes desired. This is so simple as to need no explanation.

FITTING AND LASTING THE CONGRESS.

In fitting men's congress, there are many ways of reaching the same end. Some factories believe in pasting the work all through the upper. Others use a lot of cement, and others use various machines for folding the gore edges of the lining. Again others fit and fold by hand, using no cement whatever.

It is by comparison only that we are able to arrive at proper deductions.

First fit a common cheap congress. The lining has the front seam closed, then the edges of the lining where the gore is fitted and folded or left raw edge as desired. Sometimes in a very cheap shoe it is left raw edged, and the folding is quite a disputed point. Some use a "Marshall" folder, which has a single thin steel blade, hung on to a swinging frame, rising and falling, being controlled by a treadle. This machine only folds one part, or fold, at a time, but an operator can become quite expert and work it very rapidly.

The "Shippee" folder is a "gang" machine, comprising six folders, three for each foot, and constructed so that each folds two sizes, say 9 and 10. The whole pattern must be cut specially for this machine, as the gore of a size 9 is the same size as the size 10, the difference in the leg measure being put entirely in the front and back quarters. This machine folds the entire lining, at all edges, at one operation, and does very accurate work after the patterns are fitted to it, or it to the patterns. The machine being heated, serves to keep the fold perfectly.

In other factories the edge of the lining is folded by the eye alone and with a rubbing bone, or sometimes a heated flat iron pressed so as to retain the fold. In some factories the lining is folded with the fingers, as the quarter is being stitched on. I have seen operators who had worked in this manner so long that they had become experts and could get a nice finish and do the work very rapidly. But it must have been a task to teach the operators.

The majority of those who make men's congress seem to be in favor of folding by machine. In cheap congress generally the gore is marked with a piece of red chalk, around a pattern where the quarters are to be lapped on. This gives a good guide for the operator. In some factories the lining is taken, after being seamed up the front, to the cement or pasting table, and there fitted inside the front quarter. The gore is also cemented in between the lining and outside on the front quarter. It is cemented to the back quarters in the same manner, leaving the back edges of lining and quarters open. Then it goes to the stitcher, who stitches it where the laps are. Cheap shoes are sometimes vamped, and the back seam closed clear down through lining and outside wrong-side-out, which brings the seam to the inside. Afterwards they are trimmed and rubbed, the inside back stay stitched on, covering the seam.

The quarters alone with the lining are sometimes closed, being vamped afterward. The cementer or table hand sticks the web strap in the top of the front at the time she cements and the operator on the machine places the rear web.

In fitting a fine congress the quarters will have a folded edge where they lap on the gore, and it is a matter of choice and custom whether the quarters are folded before they are stitched on the gore. They may have an allowance of a seam added, then placed on the gore wrong side up and a row of stitching put on to hold them; then rolled over on the edge and when right side up another row stitched close to the folded edge. This last method makes a very nice finish, but it needs better operators then when the edges of the quarters are folded first and then stitched on to a line on the gore.

To avoid the fullness so often seen in the front of a congress shoe, be particular as to the position of the instep on the last. This does not mean necessarily to have a different position to measure a last, but to see that the so-called waist does not extend up too far on the last on to the instep of the foot. Any shoe that is not buttoned or laced up the front will bring into prominence this fault if it exists in the last. The lining where pieced by cutting it in two pieces, lapping at the bottom of the gore, is often left loose and not sewed together. In many large factories in the East the linings are cut by dies and a beam machine. This permits many thicknesses to be cut at once and allows the cloth to be laid out the whole width. The dies are somewhat expensive, but like all such improvements are the means of making large savings daily.

When lasting congress shoes there is sometimes used a counter cut almost with square corners on the upper sides. This counter is as high as can be used between vamp seam and bottom. In lasting, the gore will stretch if the upper be pulled very hard forward. The laster sometimes pulls the shank in hard after the heel has been tacked. The counter is thus held against the vamp seam at the back of the gore. When the shoe comes off the last wrinkles will show just forward the end of the counter, showing how the counter presses up and the leather pulls down toward the shank. This indicates that the shoe has been lasted too hard down in the shank.

Observe congress shoes on the last just after they are lasted. Notice how the gore is stretched, thus allowing the forward part of the shoe to be drawn out of place by too much lasting at the outside shank. This is often shown by the curve downward in the centre of the vamp, which is generally cut on a straight line. The same often occurs in a bal if the lacing is too loose.

Another method is the cutting of a circular seam bal. generally finished with three or four rows of stitching around the quarter some three-fourths inch from the front edge and about the same distance from the back seam and top, while the lower seam is put about where the line of the top of the vamp in a whole cut.

A Creole congress is a peculiar shoe, and though not made in the finest grades, is sold in large quantities. It is

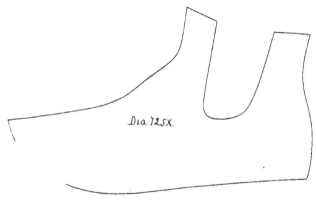

Dia. 125x.

DIAGRAM 125X.

not an expensive shoe to cut, provided large spready skins are used and competent cutters employed. Since the shoe is cut in one piece; having but the back seam it requires considerable experience and judgment to place the pattern, for the upper must not be cut from that part of the skin so as to crimp on the back and hip bones.

The pattern presented has long been in use in a factory and cuts cheaply, still leaving stock for crimping.

In cutting a new pattern it should be thoroughly tried before being accepted and adopted, for every kind of leather to be crimped needs a different allowance. It is not possible to say just where the allowance must be without trial; such matters rest a good deal with the conditions of the factory and the workmen.

It is usual in fine stock on any shoe, say kangaroo or dongola, to crimp it wrong side out, so that the grain will not be destroyed by the edge of the crimp form. Sometimes two pieces are crimped at one time, the grain sides being placed against each other.

Diagram 125X shows the cutting in pattern for the creole congress, and diagram 126X shows the blocker line.

A shows the fold, and dotted lines B C D E F show the various lines caused by swinging diagram 125X on points 1, 2, 3, as shown, after which the allowances for the taking up in crimping.

In many factories there are to be found quite a number of cutters cutting leather up into vamps, using blockers of all sizes and not throating them. At another table can be seen the "sorters," who sort up these vamps into weights, picking out at the same time the qualities, after which they are throated by other cutters. This necessitates two hand-lings and two operations of cutting.

In other factories the cutter cuts them complete, and sorts them at the same time. The latter method seems the

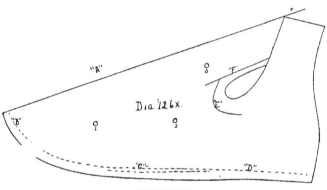

DIAGRAM 126X.

better one, for if the one cutter is expected to complete his job a little more care in cutting will be given a first-class vamp, still conditions should govern.

Again, if the cutter finishes his vamps when he first cuts them he may have two sets of vamp patterns, one to interlock, the other closed heel, working them together as he finds the stock best suited.

A good many cutters have worked in the same factory for many years and are working now just as they worked years ago, when the cost of shoemaking was not so much of an object as was the quality turned out. Now the sav-ing of trifles assures the success. How long will it take a careless cutter, or one of poor judgment, to waste his daily wages? Some of the very best and closest cutters are found in some small obscure factory in some out of the way town, and neither they nor the people they work for know they are superior workmen.

Boys' and youths' shoes are so near to men's in principle that the only difference is in height of leg and vamps; and almost no congress are made smaller than men's.

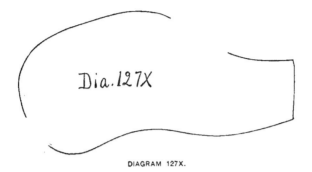

DIAGRAM 127X.

Diagram 127X shows a style of tongue for men's lace and the same is shown in diagram 128X as it should be

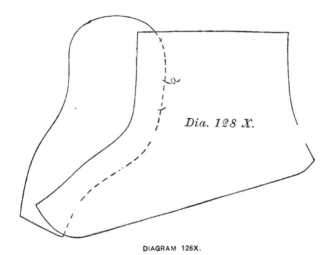

DIAGRAM 128X.

stitched to the quarter, from B to A. This tongue is one of the best for men's shoes. If put on as shown here it will draw smoothly and lay to the foot.

CHAPTER XXIII

GRADING UPPER PATTERNS.

There are several machines for grading upper patterns. Each has some claims to special merit, and several embody the best known means of obtaining widths of sole patterns. It is claimed for the improved Coté, and for the Reid machine also, that on these complete sets of all widths may be graded from one size and width of pattern. The Coté machine is adapted to grade sets of patterns by the centimeter and by the English or American systems of measurement, without any change and without extra parts.

Lasts are graded to fit the sole patterns; that is, sole patterns are got out first and the bottoms of the lasts fitted to them. But the upper patterns must be made to fit the lasts. No matter if the sole patterns are graded wrong, the lasts are made to fit them; but if upper patterns are graded wrong they will not fit the lasts. To prove that sometimes the sole patterns are graded wrong, let us grade a set only 1-16 inch across the full ball on women's shoes. The lasts are graded to fit them, but we now understand that this is wrong for anything above child's sizes. It makes the grade between sizes only 3-16 inch, leaving the larger sizes too slim in proportion to the smaller sizes, though by means of the "fan" on the last lathe a gain of on grade of one-quarter inch between sizes may be made, though the soles grade only 1-16 inch.

There is not at this writing any perfect system among last manufacturers whereby the turning lathe in different last factories turns exactly the same set of lasts from the same model. If five different last manufacturers are given the same model last to turn sets of sizes from, there is no assurance that like results will be obtained from all. Though the largest of each set may be of the same length, determined by a positive measure, called the "size stick," the girths of the largest lasts at given points are almost sure to vary. So may the smallest of the set, because the largest and smallest are the furthest away from the model size in the machine. If the turning lathe is set in different factories so as to obtain different results, that difference will be greatest in the sizes that are furthest from the model. The lathe is laid out in regular sizes in length on the levers used to set the machine, but the "fan" also regulates the grade, and different operators may bring out quite different results in lasts by adjustment of the fan.

Any one familiar with what is termed the "top switch" on upper pattern grading machines knows that although the bodies of all the machines of any one make are set to turn out like sets of patterns, different operators may make quite different sets of patterns by the way each sets the switch. This explains to some extent how the last lathe gives different results, though one unacquainted with the construction of the lathe would suppose it would give like results in all factories. Three sets of lasts in the same shoe factory produced in three different last factories, and all supposed to be turned from the same model, may be so entirely different that they could be used if mixed together and called one lot.

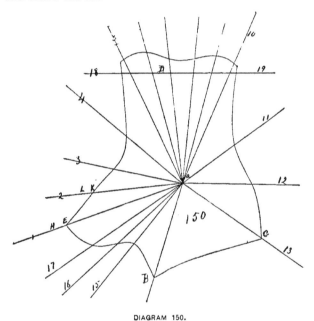

DIAGRAM 150.

When trying widths of lasts to see how they are graded, do not forget to take one of each width and place them on the table to compare the toe spring. Then try the largest of each width and see that the shank spring is uniform. Some shoe manufacturers prefer their wider width lasts longer on the toe from ball forward, commencing say at D wide 1-8 size longer, and E 1-4 size, and E E 3-8 size longer, for as the width increases the instep "fulls up" and seems to move forward, appearing to make a shorter ball. Then we get the length of the vamp on the wide widths by the addition on toe.

When grading a set of lasts, if the ball of a 4-C woman's is 2 1-2 inches across the sole, as some shoe manufacturers have it, and another 4-C is 2 3-4 inches across the ball, as other manufacturers have it, quite a difference will appear in the largest sizes of the set.

The machine for grading both sole and upper patterns which I prefer is the invention of Louis Coté, of St. Hyacinthe, P. O. Geo. W. Parrott's was the original grading machine. It is nearly forty years since he brought it out. It was not then, however, in its present perfected form.

In place of a tracing wheel on grading machines, which often becomes worn out on account of getting stuck fast, I prefer a diamond with a thin marking edge, which works equally as well on binders' board, iron, and zinc.

On the Coté machine one can do almost anything — even grade widths. The points all swing on pivot joints, and can scarcely wear so as to affect the accuracy of grading. Any height of leg may be worked on the machine, but it is arranged so that it gives the best of results on a small boot pattern where the leg is not run a regular grade.

Another machine quite well known, as the sale of it has been pushed, is the "Hartford." It is adapted to both sole and upper pattern grading.

There has also been invented a grading machine with a cutting or punching attachment that cuts the pattern as fast as it is graded.

In hand grading we have the proportional system, the 1-16 system of rules illustrated some years ago in *Shoe and Leather Record* of London, England. Then we have the "Radii" system, invented by the writer, which I will endeavor to prove is the nearest correct of any and the only one that gives the grades of the upper as demanded by the lasts. I shall show why this is so, but I do not often teach it now because it is too slow a process. These are times of push and rush, and anything that will answer and expedite in a shoe factory is adopted.

Formerly upper patterns were sometimes graded by using thick pasteboard, stacking up pieces enough for a set of whole sizes, then cutting down through all, the grade being obtained by the differential slant of the knife.

Thirty years ago a last was laid on its side on a piece of paper and a pencil drawn around it, the last in the meanwhile being rolled a little each way with the pencil. Then a pattern was gotten out and a set hand graded. After they had been tested by a manufacturer to see if they "came" pretty well, 10 or 20 sets would be gotten out, the grading being done wholly by hand. The cutting was done by tinners' straight shears, and a few carpenters' gouges. Then they were "trued up," anywhere from 1-16 to 3-16 being taken off with a carpenter's coarse rasp, after which they were bound on a small anvil with a wooden mallet. Sometimes they were run through a tinner's roll to run down the binding smoothly. Such a thing as running the binding on with a machine was not thought possible.

When grading proportional it is usual to get the pieces from the standard, having this standard as near the middle of the set to be graded as possible. In this instance we will take a 4-C woman's to start with and diagram 150. This diagram represents the large quarter of a woman's button boot. First mark around the quarter, being very careful to have the corners sharp. That will do away with the necessity of lining each side of the corner with a line from the centre. In this process it is wholly immaterial where you centre to draw radiating lines, for the result is all a matter of proportion.

CHAPTER XXIV.

If one is to hand grade one will need a pair of proportional dividers, and can pay from $2.00 to $20.00 for them; a pair costing $5.00 at the headquarters for drawing tools, are good enough. Some insist that they must be nine inches long, but while that length is convenient, equally good results may be obtained from a pair six inches in length.

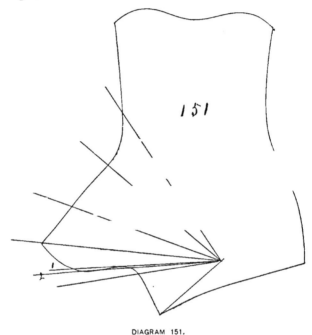

DIAGRAM 151.

The proportional divider is simply a pair of dividers with a movable fulcrum, laid off with lines and figures by which to set the line on the fulcrum. For instance it is marked 4 on a line. Now by shifting the sliding centre so that the line on which the 4 is located is even with the line on the leg of the divider, the long end when open is just 4 times as long as the short end. The short end equals just 4 spaces on the long end. So if the short end is set on 5 it is just 1-5 of the long end, and so on. These proportional dividers are generally laid out from 2 to 9 or 10, and the principle is just the same. But when commencing to grade sizes we have nothing to do with the figures on the leg. First set the long end so that one leg rests on the

point of the toe at "C," diagram 152, and the other on point
at "B." Next mark around the standard diagram 152, after
which draw the line "A" "A" from point of toe to about the
centre of heel bulge. Then find one-half, as at B, and obtain the length of the 4-C complete. Reverse the dividers
and the short end must be just 2 sizes on the size stick. Of
course it will not come the first time trying, but keep trying until the long ends will fit from "C" to "B," and the
short ends register 2 sizes on the stick.

In laying out the centre point from which to draw radiating lines, use judgment and so place it that the lines will
not cross each other in ruling, as in diagram 151, as seen at
"1"-"2."

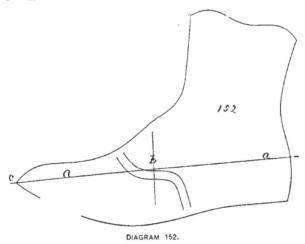

DIAGRAM 152.

This diagram is shown for explanation. At "A" you
will see how lines 1 and 2 interfere with each other, yet
otherwise one could get the same result in the finished set.
Have the quarter diagram 150 lined ready to grade.

Use diagram 150 and place a needle in what we call the
centre at "A." Draw lines sufficient to break the circles
all around. If a straight line or a continuous curve is anywhere on the pattern, only one is needed at each end, as at
the bottom of the quarter from corner to corner, "B" to
"C." Across the leg near the top draw the horizontal line
as seen at "D." At that point a positive measurement is
wanted, as grade and the dividers will not give it so correctly as they do the rest of the pattern.

Next place one long leg of the dividers in the centre
at "A," diagram 150, and on line 1 at "E."

Reverse the dividers, being careful not to move the
legs, and with the short end measure one space from "E" to
"H," diagram 150. Then measure on line 2 from centre to
intersection of quarter at "K." Reverse the dividers and

space on line 2 as at "L" and so on with 3, 4, 5, 6, 7, 8, and up to line 1.

On lines 17 and 18 mark out just 1-4 inch from quarter leg. You now have size 8, four sizes from the model.

It will be easy to understand that since you took one-half the length of the standard diagram 152 for the long end of dividers, the short end registering two sizes on the size stick, if the dividers had been long enough to have measured the entire length of the standard and the short end had measured 4 sizes the result would have been the same. So a pair of small dividers answer just as well as the larger and more expensive ones.

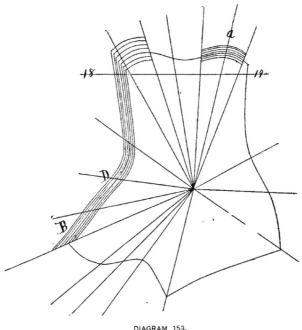

DIAGRAM 153.

Having the quarter 4 and 8 sizes, change the dividers. Set the fulcrum on 4. The short end of the dividers will be just one-fourth of the long end; reversing, and with the short end dividing between, the sizes 4, 5, 6, 7 and 8 are obtained. While the dividers are set just as they now are, run in on line 1 and get sizes 3 and 2.

For half sizes put leg of the dividers half way between the whole size in any one place, and space out and in from that point. Continue all around until reaching lines 18 and 17, when 1-16 of an inch is a whole size, on each side, as that increases or decreases the sizes just 1-8 inch, which is correct, as 1-8 inch on each quarter makes 1-4 on both and that is the same as the ball of the last changes in sizes. Diagram 153 will show the quarter spaced whole sizes and lined part of the way around.

To line from space to space use the standard 4 size, keeping the circles as near their relative position as possible. This spacing and lining is a matter of care only. Should you desire a lesser grade at the top leave it until the last of the work and then instead of setting the dividers on 4 division, you set at 6 or 8, making the grade less on top, as seen at "A," diagram 153. At the front can be seen a full grade in height.

Remember that if you use a lesser grade on the quarters in the height you must use the same on the top of the button fly, fly lining and drill lining.

One thing to be said in favor of hand grading is that all machines grade the laps on all places where the laps are left on the model pattern to work from. If it be 5-16 lap in that standard it will be considerable more on the size 7 or 8 woman's and proportionally less on the sizes under

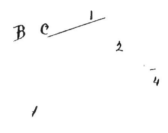

DIAGRAM 154.

the model size. One would not realize how much this throws a set of patterns out unless he grades another set with no laps allowed, and then put the laps on with the dividers. Such tests are always instructive.

Another test is to mould a last very carefully, say size 3 woman's, then get out a standard and grade in any manner; or make test grades on machines and by all known hand systems, after which mould the size 8 last as carefully as possible. Place it on standard size 8 graded up, and see how you have been following the grade of the lasts.

The trouble is that we do not grade uppers as the lasts call for, except by the Radii system, and that is too slow to use at present. The proportional system here illustrated is not correct when the requirements of the lasts are taken into consideration, as any one can see almost at a glance.

In diagram 153 at "B" the grade is really greater than at "D"; yet at "D" the last is at its fullest measurement point, and just about over the centre of the shank where scarcely any grade is in the sole. Therefore, nearly all the grade which is in the last 1-4 inch must be furnished by the two quarters, while at "B" the grade of the sole at the ball is 1-12 inch, and that means that the two quarters and the vamp at that measurement point only require 1-6 all together.

It is often observed where hand grading is practiced that the largest sizes come tightest on the last, though the soft, stretchy upper leather used nowadays permits mistakes to be made and not show as formerly when brush or Curacoa kid were all we had for women's shoes.

Do not forget that at lines 18 and 19 there is 1-16 inch grade. Grade the vamp, and as all the vamp patterns are cut folded so as to have both sides alike, fold a piece of

155

DIAGRAM 155.

paper large enough, and then mark around the half vamp as got from the working standard. Call it diagram 154, after which select the point easiest to work from as centre of radiating lines. Draw lines sufficient to break all curves. Too many lines do no injury, but only serve to make unnecessary work.

The lines as drawn in diagram 154 will apply to all ordinary circular curve vamps. It is best not to round the corners on vamps or quarters until the set is out, as all should have the same amount of stock cut off. If the rounded corners were graded the round would be greater on the larger sizes, while we expect to lap the same on all sizes, and to lose the same amount of stock in folding the edges.

Next set the dividers by diagram 152 so that the long legs register one-half the standard, as from "C" to "B,"

while the short legs register two sizes on the size stick, as
it was worked in grading the quarter. Place one long leg
in "A," diagram 154, and the other long leg in the intersection of the line 1 and the back curve of the vamp at "B."
Reverse the dividers and point off on line 1 at "C." Then
take the same method with each line 2, 3, 4, 5, 6, 7, after
which again reset the dividers on 4, or one-quarter length
on small end to the long end, as this has so far given us 4
sizes from the model. Now we have a 4 size and size 8,
and only want to sub-divide and get the intermediate sizes.

Setting on one-fourth gives one size on the short end.
Space on one size at a time, out or in, larger or smaller, as
desired. This gives spacing as may be seen on diagram
154, after which line all around with the model size as a rule
to draw the pencil against.

156

DIAGRAM 156.

The diagram is only ruled part of the way, as it shows
the spacing better. Judgment or common sense must be
exercised in meeting with other curves on vamps.

Diagram 155 illustrates this. In such a case we can
use but a half vamp, as the grade comes partly where the
paper would be folded. If one becomes accustomed to
hand grading one will not be worried should lines cross
each other so that at times one cannot cut off the grade at
the lines. Then one will only prick through and work from
the prick marks to line again. Sometimes it is almost impossible in crooked work to prevent the larger pieces in
certain locations from coming inside the smaller ones.
Practice and familiarity will set all right.

Diagram 156 shows the circular vamp with a different
centre to grade from, but it will only work on a half vamp,
as you can see, because it also grades on the fold edge.

CHAPTER XXV.

Next we will get a lining from the standard and mark
around as shown in diagram 157, after which centre and
draw radiating lines as shown, always remembering how to
increase the height of the quarters, as they must correspond; also the width of the leg. Though we are aware of
the fact that this grading is not as the lasts require it in all
ways, yet the whole set of patterns is to be used to cut shoes
from, and they must be got out so that the different parts
of the shoes will come together right in the fitting room, or

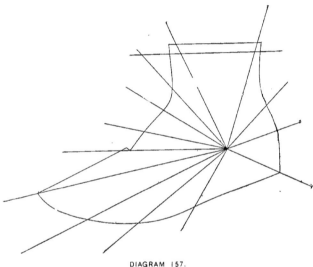

DIAGRAM 157.

there will be endless trouble. In other words the lasters
have for years pulled the shoes on the lasts so that they have
answered, but the head of the fitting department cannot get
the shoes together unless the patterns are cut so as to come
somewhere nearly right.

There probably is no use to illustrate the grading on
the lining, for the process is just the same in all the set, and
on different parts.

Next we will get the button fly as shown in diagram
158. Centre it to one side, for if centered in the centre of
the fly it will make very close work on both sides. Use 1-32

grade at "A" in front of leg, obtaining the balance of grade at back of fly.

Diagram 159 shows the full standard lined out to grade by this system, and as the process is similar to all the rest there is no necessity to space in this diagram. Any one who desires to use this proportional system should be able from these instructions to apply it to any kind of a pattern.

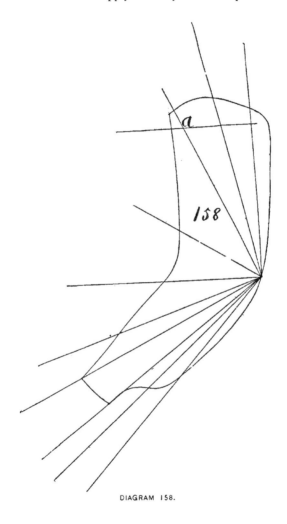

DIAGRAM 158.

All widths of women's lasts are supposed to grade the same in size, namely 1-4 inch in girth.

Conceding that the lasts are correct, that we have all widths, and that our first order calls for E E patterns, 2 1-2 to 8, first mould a 4 last and get out a standard. From that next get the quarters, vamp lining and other parts to grade from. Now a E E pattern is very much larger, of course,

than an A, as the mould of the last gives it. You are grading from a very large surface, and as the grade is by the
system in proportion to the surface graded from in all directions, a much greater grade is obtained between sizes from
a E E width than from a A A; yet the grade between the
sizes of lasts is 1-4 inch in A A and E E, both the same.

Either you get considerably too much grade from the
E E or too little from the A A last. How can you recon-
cile one to the other? Yet for years this process was accepted as correct. Thousands of sets of patterns were got
out thus, and the lasters were blamed if the shoes did not
fit. Or the trouble was laid to the fitting room.

After grading a set of patterns as above by hand, the
easiest and best way to get the set in metal or board is to

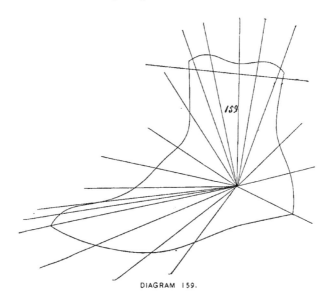

DIAGRAM 159.

cut off each piece to the outside line and then mark around
it on the metal or board with a fine awl. Then cut down
to the next size or half size and mark around that, and so
on down to the smallest. Of course this destroys your
graded paper, but you have the set ready to get out. If you
want a duplicate it is easy to mark around your set of metal
or board patterns.

The foregoing method of grading brings very much
the same result as does the method or system lately ex-
plained and illustrated by Mr. Day of London; yet there is
some difference, as for instance the proportional system as
taught by others, so far as I am acquainted, pays no attention to the results in the top of the leg, and not doing this
gives a result entirely wrong, as can be seen illustrated in
diagram 160.

You will see that the smallest size has the most flare of leg at the back at top. This is of course wrong, as it should be of the same general character clear through the set. This should hold good in all but infants', where the size o or 1 should be much fuller at the top in proportion to the rest of the shoe than size 5, which is generally supposed to end the infants' sizes.

Hand grading is the best method to use when working on infants' shoes, though a good many use the different machines and seem satisfied with results. When getting out infants' patterns mould smallest size last and get out stand-

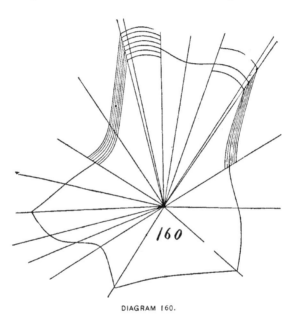

DIAGRAM 160.

ard. Then get out the largest standard from the largest last, varying in leg as deemed best, after which get the pieces of the largest size and smallest size and grade between with the proportional dividers, as this is the only method of obtaining a proper result. After a set of infants' has been graded do not allow a file put on them for trueing up, for fear of losing the small curves necessary to bring out a small shoe.

There appears no necessity of going into grading on the "proportional" system any further, as the rule is carried out in all cases.

CHAPTER XXVI

Next come to the old 1-16 inch rule used by many. It is sometimes assisted by the eye and partly combined at times with the "sliding" system, or "rule of thumb," and practice. Any one using this system with satisfaction to themselves certainly does not understand the need of lasts, for it is like some others, a system of itself, without regard to requirements. Perhaps you can fully understand what there is to it just as well without diagrams.

After getting your large quarter, mark around it and with a divider set on 1-16 of an inch, space up the front of the quarter along the instep until you reach the curve of the throat. Then space 1-8 inch up the front of the leg, when line so as to make a good joint of leg and instep lines. Down the front curve of the quarter is a matter (speaking of women's patterns) of judgment, of care on curves, of trying to reach the bottom of the quarter with a whole increase of 1-16 inch gain.

Commence say with women's patterns, as there is so much more to a woman's pattern than a man's. Men's **patterns** are composed of so few pieces, and the stock cut by them is of such a character that less definiteness in detail is needed. See that there is 1-16 on bottom. While laying out the front curve of the quarter add on the point 2-3 of a size from the size stick, to increase the length, one-third being put on the back of vamp in that particular place, and on the bottom end of curve add 1-3 size. Then in sliding the curve gradually reach from one point to the other.

In grading sizes there seems to be a great difference of ideas as to how much each size gains or loses in height. Of course the body of the patterns is regulated in grade by the lasts, but the height of the leg in grade is decided by the individual who has that part of the business to settle. Some manufacturers have the grade very small, and say that a buyer always decides on his purchase from the sample shown, which is, in woman's, generally a 3 1-2 or 4, and that they do not say anything if the larger sizes do not grade much in height. Of course if one can keep down the grade on top of the leg it will result in a large saving in upper stock. Others say they want 7 or 8 to resemble the 4 in all ways. In hand grading by any method this can be regulated according to desire; so also in using some machines. Where a shoe factory has its own equipment of pattern making it is easy after settling the point to grade all alike, but where the factory has patterns made outside in a pattern factory, one should always send a large and a small size quarter of the same set which is satisfactory, that the pattern maker can govern his grade accordingly. This is especially necessary when ordering part of a set, as is often done. Sometimes a manufacturer orders sets of linings only for the sets he has on hand in widths; and simply sends a 4-C lining to the pattern maker who did not make the original sets.

When grading lengths of the vamps, some manufacturers want only half a grade in the throat, so that the largest sizes will not run back on the instep as far as a full grade would bring them. This of course necessitates more work on the ends of the quarters, as they must be correspondingly lengthened. This is but little extra trouble if the grading be done by hand, but on the machines it involves much extra work, and on some of them it is impossible. So also as to width of top facing. Some want the same width in all sizes. The outside front facings of a front lace shoe are generally all the same width, and it is almost as easy to get them from the front of the quarter patterns and then get the widths with dividers if a plain straight facing; but if they are fancy cut on one side then it is best to grade them on the backs and use the graded set backs to get a hand grade width.

Machine grading changes the back end of the tip, if to be perforated, so that the same edge perforations will not work. In grading tips it is well to get all the grade except the back line.

CHAPTER XXVII.

ONE METHOD CORRECT.

There is one method of pattern grading, which so far as grading is concerned, is absolutely correct, and only one. By this system one can grade ten sizes, provided the lasts are graded properly that many sizes and all will fit equally well. Not only that but any last, the largest or smallest even of a set of ten sizes, may be moulded and a standard got from it, and then the entire set graded up or down from that standard with the certainty that all will fit alike.

When the system here referred to was developed the grading machine was almost unknown. In a series of experiments and tests I demonstrated the method of moulding

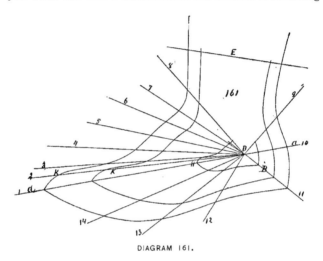

DIAGRAM 161.

a last which is set forth in the first chapter of this work. I proved that when a reasonable amount of care is used that method of moulding produces a correct result.

Having a correct method of moulding the last I next turned my attention to the grade of upper patterns as required by the lasts. I went to a last factory and selected a good model 4-C. From that I had a set of lasts made on a straight grade of 1-4 inch from 11 misses to a woman's 7. Of course this was not correct to make shoes from, but I was not making shoes, I was making experiments. I was careful in these early experiments that the lasts graded right.

After this I laid all aside but the size 11 and the woman's size 7. I had nine grades between or ten lasts. If

I could find the amount required for uppers of these nine grades I could easily find one-ninth or one grade. So I tried to get a chart of the grade. The size stick helped me for it gave a positive grade as to length. I wanted something just as positive in all directions. I had nobody's experiments in this line to assist me as all grading systems previously used were exclusive of the demands of the lasts, and mainly by "rule of thumb."

I moulded the 11 and 7 carefully getting out standards from each, caring only to have the legs pitch the same. I got the ankles from the ball measure, and left the top of the leg entirely out of the question, for that was to be a matter of taste.

I marked around the 7 standard as shown in diagram 161, and drew line "A" "A" from the point of the toe to about the centre of the heel. Then I drew line "B" from the

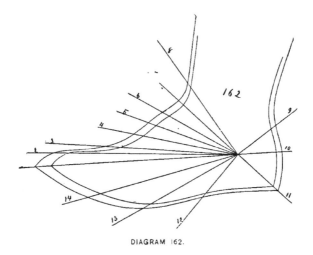

DIAGRAM 162.

corner toward the centre of the throat, but only beyond where it intersects line "A" "A."

Next I placed the size 11 standard inside of the 7, as at diagram 161, and divided the leg equally in front and back. I then marked around standard 11. Next I placed a pin in centre D and struck out radii 1, 2, 3, 4, 5, and so on up to 14. In drawing these I only looked to breaking of curves all around. Then I marked across the legs near the top, calling it E, and found that I had 9-16 between each, fronts and backs. Of course you understand that great care was taken that the upper standards 11 and 7 were just right in allowance for lasting.

Next I took the measure between the 7 and 11, on line 1, and transferred it to centre, as seen at "H." Then I took the difference at "K," line 2, and transferred it to centre, as shown; and so on, each one successively until I had the

whole 14 measures in the centre of the chart, and these
lines I termed "Radii."

Now that I had nine grades in a small chart, I could
set my proportional dividers. on 9, or one-ninth—that is
have the short legs one-ninth the length of the long legs—
when any measurement of the long legs would result in one-
ninth on the short, or nine grades on the long end would
be one grade on the short end. If I had one grade correctly it was just what I wanted.

Then I got a 4-C standard, marked around it, as seen
in diagram 162, cut mv little radii, and putting it so that
lines 1, 10 and 11 intersected, placed a pin in the centre,
holding it in position with a tack at the top. Then I drew
lines 2, 3, and 4 and so on up to 14, according as they were
on the radii. I also numbered them the same.

With my dividers on one-ninth, I took the measure of

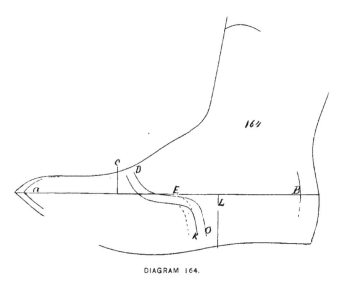

DIAGRAM 164.

line 1 on the radii on the long leg. Then I had the one
grade on the short end. So I merely run out on line 1 up
to size 7, taking measure of line 2 on the radii and run out
from size 4 up to 7. Then I took measure on line 3 and
proceeded as before. And so on around the work.

I took my 4 standard and ruled up to size 7, just as the
lasts called for it, spacing at or near the top of the leg 1-16
each size both back and front. Then I had the 4 and 7 outsides except the tops.

I laid out my vamp curve by first drawing on diagram
163 the straight line "A" "A" from point of toe to full of
bulge of heel on my size 4 standard, by taking 4 5-8 inches
from the back of the heel forward to the line B, for that
brought the end of the vamp line to the centre of the shank.

Then I measured where I wanted the top of the vamp to end for length.

I then divided the entire length of the standard on line "A A" into three equal distances, after which I drew a right angled line down at the rear one-third, as seen at D. From the front one-third I drew perpendicular line as seen at E. This gives the thirds equally divided. Now divide your largest size the same way, the straight line corresponding as to height at heel, diagram 164.

Next cut out the lap of quarter and vamp, as seen in diagram 163, II. This gives you a hole to see through.

Place the standard 163, or size 4, on size 7, diagram 164, so that the toe of the 4 will be on the straight line, as seen at A, diagram 164. The heel end of the straight lines

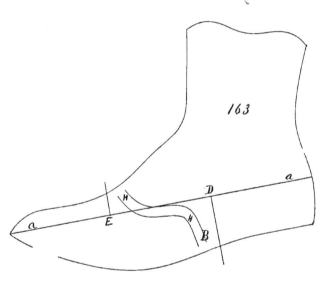

DIAGRAM 163.

should correspond, as at B, 164; and the front perpendicular lines at C should be upon one another. Then mark through the vamp from D to E, 164, a solid line, and dotted line from E to K. Next slit the 4 on the 7 until the rear perpendicular lines L are one upon the other with the straight lines upon each other. Mark down the rest of the vamp lines, as seen at O, and you will have the size 7 vamp closely corresponding with the size 4. If it should be a little out it is not detected with the eye, and if the vamp is deficient the deficiency is made up by the quarter. The entire standard or upper is correct to fit on the last.

If a foxing is desired, first lay out the foxing in the size 4 standard, and then try the means just employed in dissecting for vamp. It is much easier than it appears; but

like almost any other mechanical process, may require considerable practice to become expert.

It is the same process on a low cut, for a low cut is
nothing but a high boot with the leg cut off. We are always insured as to the fitting qualities on the last, and any
one can see that no laps are graded, but only body of the
pattern.

After getting the large size 7 quarter from the size 7
standard, and the size 4 large quarter from the size 4 standard, mark around the large one, then place the 4 inside, as
illustrated by diagram 165, dividing the difference all
around about equally, so as to make it more convenient to
grade. It will be noticed that whole sizes only are shown in

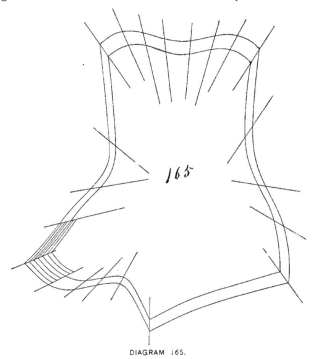

DIAGRAM 165.

diagram 165, but this was done so that the engraver of the
diagrams would not be obliged to do such fine work as half
sizes would represent.

The cross lines at the various positions from the large
to the small quarter are frequent enough only to break the
curves. Notice that we now have a size 4 and 7. Of course,
that is four sizes, or three grades. Set the proportional dividers on the one-third mark on dividers, and then with one
long leg on the 7 and the other on the 4, get the divisions
on each line. After grading from 7 to 4, run on the inside
of size 4 until the necessary smaller sizes are obtained, say
a 3 and 2.

There are lines at the toe of the quarters, as seen on diagram 165, sufficient to show the idea, and a continuation of spacing and lining is all that is required to make a full set of quarters.

Diagram 166 shows the largest and size 4 vamps laid out for grading a set on the same principle as the quarters. It is well to use the largest standard in ruling the lines, as the other would run short on all corners. Ruling across often enough to break the curves answers every purpose. In getting the rest of the set of patterns get out the 4 and

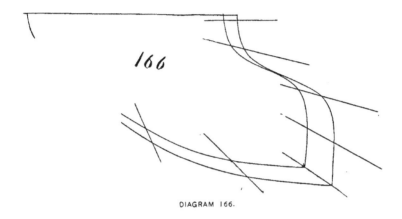

DIAGRAM 166.

7 fly and grade between. Then when getting out the top facing, if preferred, keep the whole set one width.

In fact, with this method the dissection of any and all parts is made with the positive assurance that the whole set will come together as if they had grown there, something no one can do with machine grading. Yet machine grading may be preferred because so rapid in comparison with this slow method.

A good many people are using the various machines for grading who do not thoroughly understand them, and oftentimes fail to obtain as good results as they might.

CHAPTER XXVIII

At the time I invented the Radii system, many sets of
women's and misses' lasts were turned with the 3-16 grade
in girth, and at that time one last maker in Lynn told me
that he graded children's soles 1-16 across the balls, and
misses' 1-14, and women's 1-12 of one inch. So when I
asked him how he graded the lasts he said he did not know,
but it was just as the turning lathe left them, except the finishing, which meant shaving and polishing.

Men's lasts have for a long time been graded very similar to the present grade, and there has not been very much
change in the finest grades, but the last manufacturers who
once made a specialty of peg lasts are nearly all now making efforts in the finer grades.

Grading widths is not generally well understood. There
must be some definite point settled before measurements
can be accepted. If "around the ball" means straight
around, then let it be so understood. If it means at an angle
from the inside ball to the outside ball, then let there be a
positive angle. If we have a ball measure for the foot, then
let us have a measuring position so far forward from the full
of the heel, and at a certain diagonal across the foot or last.
When a positive position is definitely settled upon let it be
applied to both the foot and last alike, so that one person
can measure the foot, and another the last, and with a certainty that they both agree in every particular.

No one should grade patterns in widths, unless he has
by some means satisfied himself that there is a certain definite grade of the lasts to be worked upon, and what that
grade is. In doing this it is necessary to know also if each
width has a sole of its own, or whether one sole answers
for more than one width, and if it does, what widths it is
used on. Not infrequently the same insole is used in making two or more sets of lasts in width, and on children's
shoes one last is often used for two widths, the only difference made in the upper pattern being in the width of ankle.

Some manufacturers use only three widths of patterns
to get six widths of shoes, and get what they seem to be satisfied with by cutting up and down, and crossing a vamp
on to a quarter and fussing and fitting.

There is nothing less expensive to a shoe manufacturer
than complete sets of lasts and complete sets of patterns,

when all things are considered, provided lasts and patterns are right.

Feet vary much in shape as well as in measurement, and were it not for the readiness by which button and lace shoes are adapted to size and shape of feet by moving the buttons and leaving the lace to adjust itself, we would have much more trouble. Few factories have lasts where any two sets are of the same rear part. That is, the parts back of the ball do not resemble each other. Then, again, in widths, how few manufacturers have insisted that all of one style shall have the same toe spring? But the wider the width, the greater the toe spring is often seen.

Again, the instep of the wider widths are liable to grow too far ahead and too prominent, thus cutting short the chance for a middling long vamp, as it would not last down on the sides. Some of our most prominent manufacturers try to overcome this difficulty by increasing the length of the last, the increase being wholly on the toe. I have found lasts that varied but 3-16 grade between widths.

A majority of the trouble in patterns is caused by taking too much for granted. A pattern that is successful in one factory may be all wrong in another factory, where conditions are different. In troubles that come upon you in this connection common sense must be the good friend who will help you out of your difficulties.

When preparing to grade widths, it is advisable, after measuring the lasts, to mould the model size of each width carefully, to be sure that all lasts of each set give similar curves in like positions. Nothing will give the pattern man a more correct idea of the work before him than a complete set of last moulds, each marked so as to be used intelligently at any time. This does away with repeated mouldings.

No man is capable of making models for lasts until he knows how to get correct standards of upper patterns from them. He may make models, but he does not know what he will get for shoes from them until he has standards.

A pattern from a last of a certain size and width should have a certain heel measure. Heel measure in a pattern is just as essential for a good fitting shoe as ball measure.

To get the heel measure of the pattern it is absolutely necessary for a last model maker to either know how to get a proper standard from any new last he may get up, or have some one near him who does know. This standard must, to a certain extent, decide if his model be correct. And the more progressive last manufacturers will do this soon.

After strapping and moulding one size of each width, it is easy enough to see what is needed in getting out patterns in widths to fit the lasts.

Pattern making has, within a few years, become a profession which requires a thoroughly practical knowledge of the fitting room. Unless the pattern maker's work is in harmony with the requirements of that room in putting uppers together, his patterns will be a failure. A pattern maker should visit the fitting room often and notice if buttons are in correct positions on the button boots.

The heel measure of a woman's pattern is reckoned from the sharpest curve of the quarter at the throat to the bottom of the last at the heel. Where the upper and counter turns under the last on a 4-C button boot this measurement should be 11 1-2 inches, and then run less on each narrower width 5-16 inch and on wider widths the increase should be 5-16, while on E width the increase should be a

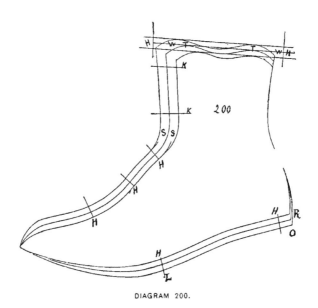

DIAGRAM 200.

little more than the 5-16, and on EE the increase would be well to be 3-8, although in regular width grading generally holds to 5-16 increase for each width.

In grading widths on the top of the leg, AA or AAA width is generally worn by a slim woman who has scarcely any swell at the calf, and the top should not be increased in proportion, whereas a woman wearing an E or EE is almost always fleshy and has a large calf, hence top of the leg should be larger than a regular grade. Of course this is not always done in grading, but any one can understand that it is likely to be proper. Again the button or lace for a fastening comes to our relief, for buttons can be moved and lacing can be left open.

The grading of widths in women's shoes is a matter of

close penciling and cutting, and is much the hardest to get out. A slight variation in men's patterns from the exact ness necessary in women's is not noticed. The lines are not so particular nor the curves of the outline so sharp and defined. Then there are so few pieces in men's to come together, whereas in women's we have many small, sharp curves. The stock used on the finer grades of women's demands more care.

Take a standard of a 4-C, diagram 200, and line around it. Grade out to EE and into AA, making three grades larger and three grades smaller than the model. This is

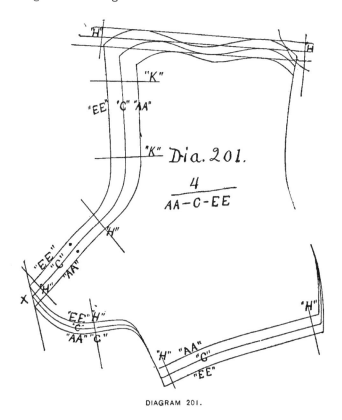

DIAGRAM 201.

shown for all the widths of lasts of the same length, but if there is increase in the wider widths in the length of toe from ball forward, simply add the extra on the toe of the wide sizes. At H space 1-16 inch for each width and at K space 1-8 inch for each width. In lining the bottom from L to O have the standard 4-C, or whatever standard you use to work from on spaces at HH. Have the fullest part of the bulge at heel at P even, so that you will get the proper curve at bottom of the heel as seen at R. If this is not done the

wider widths will be cut under at this point, and the narrower widths will be left too full at extreme bottom. The
lining of the grading of widths is so very simple and apparent that it is not necessary to dwell on it. It is best to
line up the front from the toe to curve of throat, shifting the
standard as necessary, until the throat is reached. Then the
lines will run out as shown at SS. Then line down the front
of the leg, spaced at KK 1-8 inch to each width, being
careful to guide by the spacing at KK and moving the
standard up until the throat curve strikes on the instep line
and the two make a continuous line.

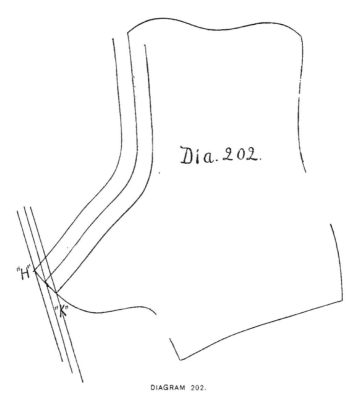

DIAGRAM 202.

At the top of the leg draw a horizontal line W, resting
on the two highest points as at TT, and draw it away beyond the leg at each side. Then space up and down for
each width as much as you please.

A space of 1-16 inch is generally preferred. If the
shoes must be cut cheaply as possible, it is well sometimes
to keep all the larger widths the same height and grade
none, grading down the narrower widths. Such matters
are to be governed entirely by conditions.

By these general rules widths will all have a family re-
semblance, and, provided your men's, boys', women's and

misses' lasts are graded 1-4 inch in width and the soles 1-12 inch, the patterns will fit all widths alike.

Diagram 201 shows the quarter graded from 4 C to 4 EE down to 4 AA. Up the instep, across the top, on the bottom and down the back, the grading in widths is the same as in standard diagram 200. The front of the quarter is graded in this diagram so as to have all widths of quarters the same length.

Diagram 202 shows the same 4 C quarter graded up to a 4 EE and down to a 4 AA in the way many pattern makers are now grading. It must necessarily cause the 4 EE quarter to grow longer as seen at H and shorter on the AA as seen at K, diagram 202. The result of this method of grading in width is not often noticed by any one who is not "up" in the knowledge of patterns, and is so much less work than the method shown in diagram 201.

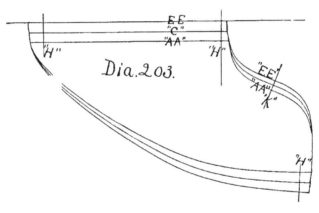

DIAGRAM 203.

In diagram 202 it will be noticed that the point of the quarter grows wider on wide widths and narrower on narrow widths very rapidly, too rapidly to look well. The method shown in diagram 201 is better. In this, as may be seen, a perpendicular line has been drawn on the point of quarter at X. Notice that the EE and AA quarters end at the same line, thus keeping them all of equal length. Also you will see that the throat of the vamp increases only 1-16 inch to the width as it is also graded at line G 1-32 inch to the width.

There are other methods used by pattern makers in grading widths, but it seems unnecessary to illustrate further. One method used by many, results in throwing the legs of the different sizes further forward or back, as the case may be, consequently the legs of the shoes in different sizes do not stand with like pitch.

In the width grading system here described I have been entirely guided by the lasts, but have likewise made free use of common sense—a necessity to successful pattern making.

In lining down the front curve of the quarters, it is necessary to keep the standard quarter by which you work in alignment, for if it is twisted your curves will not harmonize. In diagram 203 is shown the vamp graded from a 4 C to 4 EE, and 4 AA showing as in the previous widths only the extreme and the standard 4 C. At HHH the grade is 1-16 inch and at K it is only 1-32 inch. It is only graded in one-half vamp, so as to cut on fold line. This

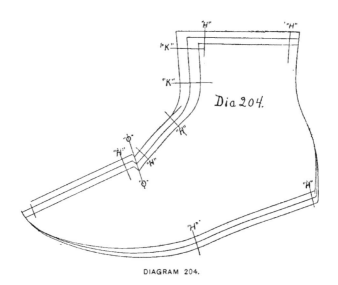

DIAGRAM 204.

grading is illustrated so plainly in diagram 203 as to preclude the necessity of further explanation.

Next refer to diagram 204 for explanation of grade in the width of lining pattern. At HHH the grade is 1-16 inch and the grade at K is 1-8 inch, while at O the perpendicular line retains the same length of lining where it meets the quarter, for lining and quarter must compare. The front of the lining is graded to match the grade of the vamp. Notice that at the back of the heel near the bottom the grade is the same as the quarters.

CHAPTER XXIX.

GRADING BUTTON FLY.

Probably the most difficult part of width grading has been the button fly. To illustrate this properly will require a few extra diagrams, but as the result is so satisfactory it is well to go to the bottom of the matter. In the first place we will grade and cut each quarter in the various widths desired, to get the fronts of the flys, by marking around the quarters at top front, and a short way along the bottom ends

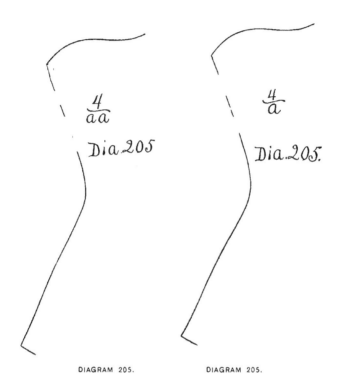

DIAGRAM 205.   DIAGRAM 205.

of the front or instep line, leaving plenty of paper back of the front lines. Cut out each button fly as far as lined; see diagrams 205 AA, A, B, C, D, E, EE.

Next cut these flies out, on the lines, leaving plenty of stock back, so that they resemble diagrams 205, being cut on the lines. Next get, say, a duplicate of a 4 C fly as shown in diagram 205, and then cut the back of it to suit the requirements as to sweep, width, etc.

Next place the fly so cut in front as seen in diagram

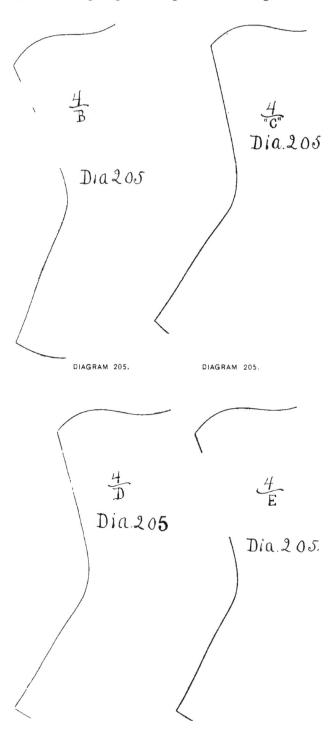

$\frac{4}{B}$

Dia 205

$\frac{4}{\text{"C"}}$

Dia. 205

DIAGRAM 205.   DIAGRAM 205.

$\frac{4}{D}$

Dia. 205

$\frac{4}{E}$

Dia. 2 05.

DIAGRAM 205.   DIAGRAM 205.

206 one upon the other, with the space down the front of
the leg to suit your own ideas regarding the grade of each
width. If an opinion has not been formed place them 1-16
inch from the edges of each other, as the 4 C is about one-
half the width of the leg. Grade the legs in width 1-16 inch,
being careful to keep the front equidistant until the throat
curve is reached. Just below that we will reduce the grade
a trifle by sliding each up and down on a perpendicular line,
until we have reached the grade we desire on the instep line.
Then, holding all firmly in place, drive a needle through the

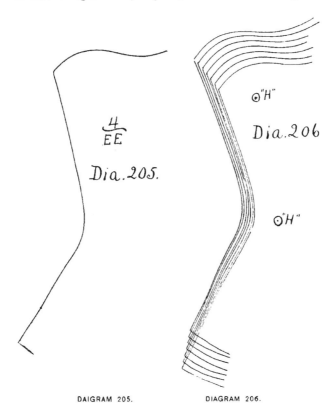

DAIGRAM 205.   DIAGRAM 206.

two marked HH. Of course, afterwards, they may all be
placed in the original position if desired by sticking two pins
through them all.

Again place the flies one upon the other, the widest
being at the bottom, and the backs not yet cut to line as
seen in diagram 207. Have the lower ends lying back, one
upon the other about 1-32 inch, more or less, as may be desired, and up the instep a little further, as seen in diagram
207, after which drive the needles through the places
marked "K." Now you remove them all, and taking your
original, which in this instance is a 4 C, lay it down on the

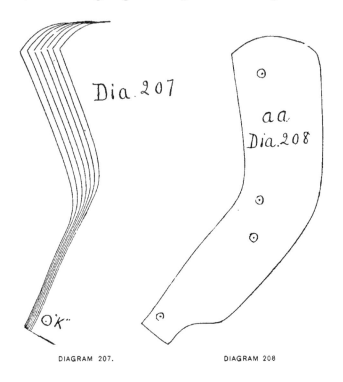

DIAGRAM 207.   DIAGRAM 208

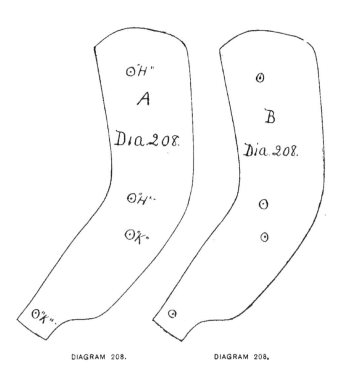

DIAGRAM 208.   DIAGRAM 208.

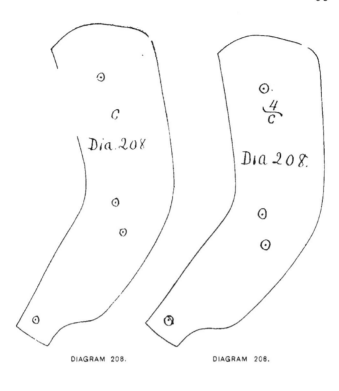

C
Dia. 208

$\frac{4}{C}$
Dia 208.

DIAGRAM 208.

DIAGRAM 208.

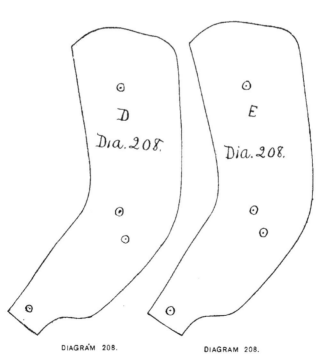

D
Dia. 208.

E
Dia. 208.

DIAGRAM 208.

DIAGRAM 208.

board, and then lay the 4 C, 205, with holes pricked at HH, and KK and having the front, top and bottom directly under the 205, mark through the prick holes. Now your 4 C original is all ready to get the corresponding curve of back on each width.

Next take EE, 205, and push the pins through the original 4 C and down through the corresponding holes HH in the EE, after which mark around the back of the original 4 C on the EE a little more than half way down the whole length. Next repeat the operation with the pins in holes KK. Afterwards use the 4 C to finish the top of back. Repeat the operation with each width, and then cut the back of each.

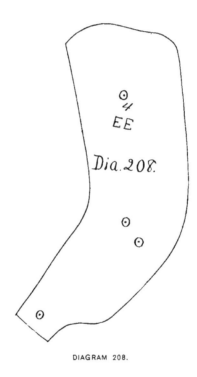

DIAGRAM 208.

See the best results of width grading of flies as shown in diagram 208 AA to EE.

There are those who after much experience grade widths by a little slipping and the use of the eye.

It seems hardly necessary to show the grading in widths of top facings, as they are generally kept all the same in width and merely grade in their length. The same may be said as to the fly linings as they are generally got from the flies. If a small lining is wanted, or if using a large and small lining pattern, which seems advisable if the conditions of the factory will permit, it is best to cut them both at once, for a double thickness of paper is cut just as quickly as a single. Then reduce the front line to correspond with the small quarter. Then, too, when both are cut at once they are of necessity exact duplicates. It would seem as though the ordinary man could from these hints apply the system to all width grading. Common sense is a great factor in width grading, but one must be careful to see that the lasts grade correctly. If one intends grading in widths it is very convenient to have a set of spacing points made from sheet steel, and arranged as follows, to be ready for any emergency: 1-32, 1-16, 1-12, 3-32, 1-6, 1-8, 3-16, 1-4, 5-16 and 1-3 inch.

Have them made very perfect at first, then you may always depend on them, and much time is saved that would be expended in setting dividers. In laying out the fly to be scalloped, it is best to lay out the top and bottom scallop first with eye, by the aid of a copper cent, or a dime, after which see how deep your chisel cuts, then set the divider and lay out the number of scallops you desire.

Some pattern makers grade widths of vamps on the grading machines. This saves time, but is not always correct, as may be proved by cutting the largest vamp of each width in paper carefully from the patterns, then just as carefully cut the quarters in paper and test the fit, comparing with the model size and width. Use paper to test anything of this kind, for one cannot get a proper test by trying the bound pieces.

Low cuts can be graded one width each way from the model width so they will work fairly well on the lasts, but you will probably find they increase too rapidly in height at the rear or heel of quarters. In using the machine for grading low cuts in widths, you grade on the same principle used in grading soles in widths.

[THE END.]

APPENDIX.

CONVENIENT RACK FOR PATTERNS.

The diagram here shown is an arrangement of pigeon holes, for patterns. Each set is supposed to have a distinct number, and any set, no matter how many there may be, may be placed in a moment by an entire stranger to the system, as well as by one accustomed to it. The extreme simplicity of the arrangement is apparent.

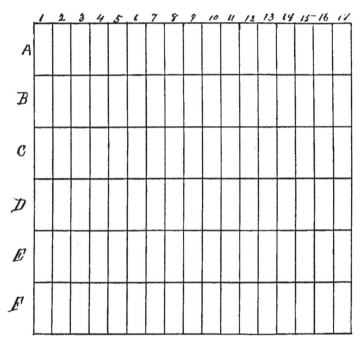

Each pigeon hole is numerically numbered at the top, while at the end the letters A B C D, and so on, represent all on that line. In a small memorandum book hanging in immediate proximity is recorded the number of each set, commencing with the lowest. Suppose we want to find set No. 21. We look in book at 21, and see it is in "5-C." Now we look at pigeon hole on line of figure 5, and then cross over at "C," and we have it. No. 181 set is wanted. We find in the indexed book that it is at "12-B." We look on line of holes 12, and where it intersects "B" we find the set.

INDEX

Index. — *Continued*.

CPSIA information can be obtained at www.ICGtesting.com
Printed in the USA
BVOW06s0836101016

464620BV00021B/191/P

9 781332 119899